MOHOMED ALI JINNAH

AN AMBASSADOR OF UNITY

MOHOMED ALI JINNAH

AN AMBASSADOR OF UNITY

HIS SPEECHES & WRITINGS

1912-1917

BY

SAROJINI NAIDU

GYAN

Published by

GYAN

Gyan Publishing House
5, Ansari Road
Daryaganj, New Delhi-110002
Phone: 011-47034999, 9811692060
E-mail: books@gyanbooks.com

Distribution Network
gyanbooks.com
India, USA, Canada, UK, Australia

ISBN: 978-93-6433-564-5 (PB)
First Published, 1917

2nd Impression 2024

Printed at: Gyan Press, Delhi.

MOHOMED ALI JINNAH
AUTHOR: SAROJINI NAIDU

MOHOMED ALI JINNAH

AN AMBASSADOR OF UNITY

MOHOMED ALI JINNAH

AN AMBASSADOR OF UNITY

HIS SPEECHES & WRITINGS

1912—1917

WITH A BIOGRAPHICAL APPRECIATION

BY

SAROJINI NAIDU

AND A FOREWORD

BY

THE HON'BLE THE RAJAH OF MAHMUDABAD

GANESH & CO., MADRAS.

"*By thine own Soul's law learn to live*
And if men thwart thee take no heed,
And if men hate thee have no care,
Sing thou thy song and do thy deed,
Hope thou thy hope and pray thy prayer."

CONTENTS.

NOTE.

The brief biographical study entitled "An Ambassador of Unity" which prefaces this volume of the Hon'ble Mr. Mohomed Ali Jinnah's speeches was originally intended for the "Indian Nation Builders" series, and claims to be no more than a hasty and imperfect sketch of a remarkable personality, meant to take its place in that little national portrait gallery of impressionist drawings of distinguished men.

My cordial thanks are due to the many friends who have afforded me their ready assistance in retrieving from scattered sources, these valuable speeches, which, now collected for the first time, cannot fail to arouse profound and vivid interest in the minds of all who are concerned with the vital issues of contemporary political events and activities in India.

To my illustrious compatriot the Raja Saheb of Mahmudabad I am deeply indebted for the admirable and characteristic Foreword which he has so kindly contributed. No token of appreciation of a man's personal worth or public work could be more appropriate or auspicious than so fine a tribute from this great-hearted Prince of Indian Nationalists to the patriotic mission of an acknowledged "Ambassador of the Hindu-Muslim Unity."

6th February, 1918. SAROJINI NAIDU.

FOREWORD.

Nothing could have given such grace and distinction to this book as the fact that that gifted lady, high priestess and soul-stirring songstress of Nationalist India, Mrs. Sarojini Naidu has sponsored it. It is no ordinary tribute to the talents, no less than to the public life of the Hon'ble Mr. Mohomed Ali Jinnah. It is certain that the lofty ideals of patriotism to which the collected speeches give witness must have swayed the minds of a larger public who read them than the audiences to whom they were addressed; but their incorporation in a more permanent and easily accessible form was eminently called for in view of what may be called the approaching final stage of the "Ambassador's Mission."

The speeches reveal a study, in a spirit of abiding and inextinguishable faith, of the problems affecting the political destiny of India, of which no other worker among the Indian Mussalmans has so far given proof in an equal degree.

It would be difficult to apportion to any one man his share of contribution in bringing about the new outlook of young Muslim India. But Mr. Jinnah's share is certainly not inconsiderable.

The reader will note one thing. The author of these speeches so aptly and so happily called "the Ambassador of Hindu-Muslim Unity," is no apostle of frenzy. Whatever success he has gained in his mission has been entirely due, at least so far as his constructive work is concerned, to arguments and facts dispassionately put forward and discussed in a calm and logical manner. Decisions arrived at in a frenzy of enthusiasm have in most cases only an evanescent existence. I do not say that the lives of nations, least of all of us Indians, are or ought to be governed entirely by cold calculating reason. The springs of emotions and enthusiasms are perennial in the Indian heart, and it is to them that Mrs. Naidu makes such instinctive, such deep and it does one's heart good to see such fruitful appeal in her splendid political work.

Mr Jinnah does not despise them ; but he leaves it to others, and his ambition seems to be to concentrate on solid arguments and concrete facts. We among Mahomedans require many more like him. My own obligations to him for this aspect of his character in the recent public life, especially of Mussalmans, are great.

LUCKNOW, 30—1—1918. | MOHAMED ALI MOHAMED of Mahmudabad.

MOHOMED ALI JINNAH.

AN AMBASSADOR OF UNITY.

A PEN PORTRAIT.

"It is my ambition to become the Muslim Gokhale," confessed Mohomed Ali Jinnah in a priceless moment of self-revelation.

In the light of this avowal it is interesting to recall Gokhale's own prediction about his gifted comrade in the service of India.

"*He has true stuff in him,*" he said, "*and that freedom from all sectarian prejudice which will make him the best ambassador of the Hindu-Muslim Unity.*"

These words, generous as they sound, are no more than a just tribute to a distinguished patriot who has so swiftly and so securely won his acknowledged place in the forefront of the national movement.

Few figures of the Indian Renaissance are so striking or so significant; to a student of psychology none more singularly attractive by the paradox of a rare and complex temperament, of strange limitations and subtle possibilities, that hides the secret of its own greatness like a pearl within a shell.

Never was there a nature whose outer qualities provided so complete an antithesis of its inner worth. Tall and stately, but thin to the point of emaciation, languid and luxurious of habit, Mohomed Ali Jinnah's attenuated form is the deceptive sheathe of a spirit of exceptional vitality and endurance. Somewhat formal and fastidious, and a little aloof and imperious of manner, the calm hauteur of his accustomed reserve but masks for those who know him, a naive and eager humanity, an intuition quick and tender as a woman's, a humour gay and winning as a child's—Pre-eminently rational and practical, discreet and dispassionate in his estimate and acceptance of life, the obvious sanity and serenity of his worldly wisdom effectually disguise a shy and splendid idealism which is of the very essence of the man.

II

Hindu by race and Muslim by religion—it may not be wholly idle to fancy something a little symbolic in the Khoja parentage of a child destined to become "an Ambassador of the Hindu-Muslim Unity."

Mohomed Ali Jinnah was born on the 25th December 1876—(there is no reliable record of the actual year)—the eldest son of a rich merchant of Karachi. Reared in careless affluence and adored by his family, he might so easily have grown into an indolent and ignorant boyhood. But he fortunately loved his studies and received his early education at the Madrassah and afterwards at the Mission School of his native city. In 1892 he was sent to England—"a tall thin boy in a funny long yellow coat,"—is an amusing description of him. There he joined Lincoln's Inn, studied law and was in due course called to the bar. It seems a pity that so fine an intelligence should have denied itself the hall-mark of a university training. But he had, instead, what from an Indian standpoint was the golden privilege of close association with the great

Dadabhai Naoroji, then President of the London Indian Society, and the guardian angel of young India in England. Who can exaggerate the value of such a noble inspiration in moulding the soul of a disciple so reverent and responsive?

On his return to India in 1896 Mohomed Ali Jinnah found his family involved in heavy financial ruin; and this favourite of fortune, suddenly faced with unexpected poverty, set out to conquer the world equipped with nothing but the charmed missiles of his youth, his courage and his ambition.

After three years of severe hardship, his brave and buoyant patience bore fruit. Through the kind offices of an old friend he was granted permission to read in the Chambers of Mr. Macpherson, then acting Advocate-General of Bombay,—a courteous concession, the first of its kind ever extended to an Indian which its recipient still remembers as a beacon of hope in the dark distress of his early struggles.

Occasional briefs now began to dribble in, and the obscure young lawyer needing only an opportunity soon proved his real mettle and started to lay the foundation of his notable legal success.

In 1906 when I met him in Calcutta at the historic Sessions of the National Congress where Dadabhai Naoroji first enunciated the glorious ideal of Self-Government for India, Mohomed Ali Jinnah, for the moment acting as private secretary to his old master, was already accounted a rising lawyer and a coming politician. For, true to his early teaching, and fired no doubt by the virile patriotism of men like the late Mr. Badruddin Tyabji and the lion-hearted Pherozeshah Mehta he had long since joined the ranks of the National Congress and regularly attended its annual gatherings. Incidentally it is interesting to note that his maiden speech at this National Assembly was made in connection with the Wakf-i-ala-aulad—a measure that was later to bring his name into such prominence. Interesting too, and suggestive in view of succeeding events, is it to find this future leader of the Mussalmans present as a sort of "crossbencher" at the Conference of Hindu and Muslim leaders convened at Allahabad in 1910, under Sir William Wedderburn's benign direction to consider a somewhat premature and artificial *entente cordiale* between the two communities still so sharply divided by a gulf of mutual dislike and distrust.

In the autumn of 1910 he was elected by the Mussalmans of the Bombay Presidency as their representative to the Supreme Legislative Council, and though the question, naturally arises as to how far it was consistent with the avowed principles of so staunch a nationalist to represent a purely sectarian interest—the fact nevertheless remains that Mohomed Ali Jinnah invariably lent his willing support to every liberal measure involving the larger national issues like Gokhale's Elementary Education Bill, for instance, and Mr. Basu's Special Marriage Bill, to which conservative India as a whole was so violently opposed. His only original work, however, during this period was in connection with the Wakf Validating Bill, to introduce which he was specially nominated for an extra term in

1913 by Lord Hardinge, then Viceroy. His admirable skill and tact in piloting through such an intricate and controversial measure—the first instance of a Bill passing into legislation on the motion of a private member—won him not only the appreciation of his colleagues but also his first meed of general recognition from his co-religionists all over India, who while still regarding him a little outside the orthodox pale of Islam were so soon to seek his advice and guidance in their political affairs.

On his return from the Imperial Council in March, he gave his evidence before the Public Services Commission then sitting in Bombay—a refreshing page in a vast mass of weary details.

* * * * *

III

Meanwhile the Time-spirit, so busy altering world-values and world-visions, had been secretly at work, and the heart of Muslim India, always passionately faithful to its own spiritual traditions, became suddenly and vividly aware also of its own political inheritance and its own responsibility in shaping the national future.

The All-India Muslim League, started a few years previously at Dacca to voice current Mussalman opinion and aspiration, was found to be too narrow and too nebulous in its scope and aims for this intense and growing national consciousness. And about the middle of 1912 a Conference of Muslim Leaders met at Calcutta to consider the remodelling of its constitution on more progressive and patriotic lines. It was decided to send Mr. Syed Wazir Hassan, the indefatigable Honorary Secretary of the League, on an extensive tour to ascertain the views of Muslims in every province regarding so momentous a change of policy and perspective. And in the following December a special council meeting of the association was called, presided over by His Highness the Agha Khan to discuss the draft of an entirely new constitution, which was ultimately and enthusiastically adopted at the memorable sessions of the All-India Muslim League held at Lucknow on the 22nd March 1913—a date that inaugurates a new era in the political history of Muslim India.

Mohomed Ali Jinnah, pledged to the greater national welfare, had with characteristic independence and honesty kept apart from a movement till then so frankly and exclusively sectarian in its purpose. But by an act of courtesy which was in itself a graceful acknowledgment of his merits he was invited to attend the Calcutta Conference, and also the later Council meeting, where being specially requested to speak, he gave his informal and invaluable support to Clause D of the new Constitution which materially embodies the Congress ideal of

"*Attainment under the ægis of the British Crown of a system of Self-Government suitable to India through constitutional means, by bringing about, amongst others, a steady reform of the existing system of administration by promoting national unity, by fostering public spirit among the people of India, and by co-operating with other communities for the said purpose.*"

* * * * *

IV

The year 1913 stands out as a distinct landmark in my friend's inner life. Not only did a wider measure of public recognition wake in him a deeper sense of personal responsibility, but one or two new and sympathetic influences brought an intimate touch of warmth and colour into his somewhat lonely and impersonal existence.

About the middle of April, he proceeded to Europe in search of a long idle holiday with Gokhale for fellow traveller, and the Arabian stars and Egyptian waters keep record, doubtless of their mutual hopes and dreams for the country of their devoted service.

Once in England, however, there was no rest for this tireless worker. He was at once drawn into the tangled web of the Indian student-world whose cause he espoused with such assiduous zeal and understanding. Within a few weeks of his arrival he founded the London Indian Association which forms so excellent a focus for the otherwise scattered energies and activities of young India in a foreign land; and it was mainly at his instance that a committee was appointed by the India Office to inquire into the legitimate grievances of Indian students suffering so keenly from an unnecessary and unaccountable set of new rules and restrictions hindering their admission into educational centres hitherto so hospitable and so easy of access.

On the eve of his departure for India in the autumn of 1913 at the express desire of his friends Messrs Mohomed Ali and Syed Wazir Hassan then in England Mohomed Ali Jinnah formally enrolled himself as a member of the All-India Muslim League to whose expanded outlook he had already contributed so signally by his example. Typical of his exquisite if somewhat exigent sense of honour is it to find that even so simple an incident partook of something like a sacrament. His two sponsors were required to make a solemn preliminary covenant that loyalty to the Muslim League and the Muslim interest would in no way and at no time imply even the shadow of disloyalty to the larger national cause to which his life was dedicated.

In May 1914 he returned to England as a member of the All-India Congress Deputation concerning the proposed reform of the India Council. He had already in this connection moved resolutions both at the Karachi sessions of the Congress a few months earlier and at the Agra sessions of the Muslim League.

In a country where the personal element forms so integral a part of public success, it was no small compliment to Mohomed Ali Jinnah's social as well as mental qualities that he was chosen to be the spokesman of articulate India before the representatives of the British Parliament and the British public. The leading English journals published numerous interviews and his concise and lucid statement of the Indian case which appeared in the London "Times" attracted widespread attention and comment.

* * * * *

V.

The tragic death of Gopal Krishna Gokhale in February 1915 brought Hindus and Mussalmans close together in a bond of common loss and sorrow. It was keenly felt that the time was now ripe for a more direct and definite *rapprochement* between the two great communities that had so recently exchanged such cordial expressions of goodwill and fellowship from afar.

The Indian National Congress was to hold its sittings that year in Bombay and there could be no better centre of reconciliation than this cosmopolitan capital of India.

Mohomed Ali Jinnah, supported at that time by all the leading local Mussalmans, sent an invitation to the All-India Muslim League to hold its next annual sessions in Bombay during the national week in December.

The story of that invitation and its startling sequel is too well-known to be retold in all the details of its shameful and subterranean intrigue so carefully conceived, so cleverly manipulated. Sufficient to say that in an hour of such grave and bitter crisis, calculated to shatter the master-dream of Indian nationalism this dauntless soldier of unity rose to the heights of an invincible patriotism. With a proud and splendid indifference, to all personal suffering and sacrifice heedless alike of official dissuasion or disfavour, the aggressive malice and machinations of his opponents or even the temporary injustice of distant friends, Mohomed Ali Jinnah strove with an incomparable devotion and courage to create that supreme moment in our national history which witnessed the birth of a new India, redeemed and victorious in the love of her united children.

Seldom has the pageant of Time unrolled a scene so touching, so thrilling, so magnificent with drama and destiny as was enacted on the afternoon of the 30th December 1915, when amidst the tears and applause of a gathered multitude the veteran heroes of the National Congress entered in a body to greet and bless their comrades of the Muslim League.

The new year dawned cloudless for this valiant fighter of national battles, bringing him some of the highest awards of his professional and public career. He added much lustre to his forensic reputation by his masterly conduct of two sensational law-suits that aroused deep interest throughout the country, connected respectively with Mr. Horniman, the trusted friend, and Mr. Tilak, the beloved tribune of the Indian people.

In the autumn he was once more elected by the Mussalmans of his province to the Viceregal Council where he commands unanimous respect and esteem by his personal dignity of character and his fearless and vigilant championship of Indian rights and demands.

Towards the close of 1916 Mohomed Ali Jinnah was twice called upon to make a public declaration of his political creed, as President of the Bombay Provincial Conference held at Ahmedabad in October, and two months later, as President of the All-India Muslim League at Lucknow.

Both his Gujarat address, in which he indicated a tentative system of administrative reforms partly based on Gokhale's scheme, since published, and in his Lucknow pronouncement where he so firmly and clearly defined the place and purpose of Muslim India in the national regeneration he proved the remarkable breadth and boldness of his statesmanship, his consummate grasp of both the transitional phases and the abiding principles of political evolution, and his incorruptible faith in the vision of a free and federated India claiming her honoured place and making her matchless contribution in the mighty republic of world-nations and civilisations.

As a speaker Mohomed Ali Jinnah has the triple assets of a magnetic presence, an impressive delivery, and a voice which while lacking volume has an arresting timbre. But though occasionaly he has attained a moment of wholly unconscious and stirring eloquence, he has the cogent force of a brilliant advocate rather than the glowing fervour of a brilliant orator. And it is not on a public platform, but at a round table conference that he finds full scope for his unusual powers of persuasion, luminous exposition, searching argument and impeccable judgment. It is an open secret that his was a large and responsible share in the recent discussions regarding the Muslim University as well as the anxious deliberations of the joint Congress League Committee that sat at Lucknow last year to formulate a scheme of Indian reforms elaborated from the Memorandum of the Nineteen.

There was, it must be admitted, a growing surprise and reproach in the minds of his followers that so ardent an apostle of Indian Self-Government should hold aloof from the recently organised Home Rule movement which was rousing the country like a clarion call to freedom. It may have been partly due to a lingering sense of allegiance to a school of politics in which he had been trained, but whose timid aud stationary doctrines he had long since outgrown or it may have been due to the habitual caution of a nature slow to commit itself to new and far-reaching responsibilities However, the news of Mrs. Besant's internment last June, which evoked such unparalleled demonstrations throughout India, moved Mohomed Ali Jinnah to a prompt and militant chivalry in defence of the immutable laws of justice and liberty so rashly and so ruthlessly assailed. He immediately joined the Bombay Home Rule League not merely as a member, but undertook, as its president, the delicate task of guiding its fortunes and guarding its interests through that troubled period of its indignant activities.

* * * * *

VI

To attempt at this stage more than a brief general survey of Mohomed Ali Jinnah's work were both untimely and unfair to a man in the very prime of life and on the threshold of his public achievement.

A casual pen might surely find it easier to describe his limitations than to define his virtues. His are none of the versatile talents that make so many of his contemporaries justly famed beyond the accepted circle of their daily labours. Not his the gracious gifts of mellow scholarship, or rich adventure or radiant conversation; not his the burning passion of philanthropy or religious reform. Indeed by his sequestered tastes and temperament Mohomed Ali Jinnah is essentially a solitary man with a large political following but few intimate friendships, and outside the twin spheres of law and politics he has few resources and few accomplishments.

But the true criterion of his greatness lies not in the range and variety of his knowledge and experience but in the faultless perception and flawless refinement of his subtle mind and spirit; not in a diversity of aims and the challenge of a towering personality but rather in a lofty singleness and sincerity of purpose and the lasting charm of a character animated by a brave conception of duty and an austere and lovely code of private honour and public integrity.

The tale of his actual contribution is still comparatively slender. But it is not by the substance but by the rare significance of his patriotic service that he holds to-day his unique place in the front rank of our national leaders.

Like others of our generation, he suffers from a system of education so widely separated from the familiar traditions and culture of our race, and lacking the magic of a common medium, he may never perhaps hope to establish between himself and his people that instinctive and inviolable kinship that makes the interned Mohomed Ali for instance, a living hero of the Mussalmans and Mahatma Gandhi a living idol of the masses.

But it is none the less his personal triumph and a testimony to his authentic mission that he stands approved and confirmed by his countrymen not merely as an ambassador, but as an embodied symbol of the Hindu-Muslem Unity.

Who can foretell the secrets of to-morrow? Who foresee the hidden forces that sometimes work to build our destiny higher than our dream? Perchance it is written in the book of the future that he whose fair ambition it is to become the Muslim Gokhale may in some glorious and terrible crisis of our national struggle pass into immortality as the Mazzini of the Indian Liberation.

HYDERABAD, DECCAN,
November 1917.

SAROJINI NAIDU

ALL INDIA MOSLEM LEAGUE, 1916.

In presiding over the All India Moslem League held at Lucknow in 1916, the Hon'ble Mr. Jinnah spoke as under:—

LADIES AND GENTLEMEN.—No mere conventional words are needed on my part to express my deep thanks for the great privilege you have conferred on me by selecting me as President of the Ninth Annual Sessions of the All-India Moslem League. The honour is the highest in the gift of the Moslem community, to which those alone may aspire, who have given freely of their thought and time to the service of the communal cause. I am fully sensible of how little I have done to deserve such distinction, nor could I have the presumption to desire it with such a clear sense of my own unworthiness. This choice, however, has come to me in the nature of a mandate from my community and in such cases individual considerations cannot and must not stand in the way of the Larger Will. I accept the great and heavy responsibilities of the position only in the belief that I can unreservedly count on your sympathy, zeal and ready co-operation in the great task that lies before us.

As President of the Bombay Presidency Provincial Conference, which was held at Ahmedabad only a few weeks ago, I have had to make a pronouncement; but at the time I accepted the honour of presiding over the Conference, I did not know that I should have this unique honour and responsibility of expressing my views as your President again within so short a time. Much of the ground was covered by me in that speech of mine. I do not now wish to repeat what I said then, nor do I wish to deal with many great and burning questions and problems that affect India in its internal administration. They will, no doubt, be placed before you in the form of resolutions which will be submitted by the speakers in charge of them for your deliberation and consideration. At the present moment the attention of the country at large is entirely concentrated and solely rivetted on the War and what will happen after the War. I have, therefore, decided mainly to deal with the situation in my Presidential address on those lines, and I will endeavour to place before you my humble views for your consideration, at the same time hoping and trusting that my feeble voice may reach those who hold the destinies of India in their hands.

ANNUAL STOCK-TAKING

In this great annual meeting of representative Musalmans from all parts of India, who have come to deliberate and take counsel together on the large and important issues that govern our destiny in this land, it will not be out of place to take a wide survey of the conditions in which our lot is cast. This is primarily the time for annual stock-taking, for testing our position in the light of the experience of the past year, for an intelligent preparation of ways and means for meeting the demands of the future, and, above all, for refreshing, so to speak, the ideals that feed the springs of our faith, hope and endeavour. This I take to be the fundamental object for which the annual sessions of political bodies like the All-India Moslem League are held. The circumstances, however, in which we meet to-day, are exceptional and mark a new epoch in the history of our country. All that is great and inspiring in the common affairs of men, for which the noblest and most valiant of mankind have lived and wrought and suffered in all ages and all climes, is now moving India out of its depths. The whole country is awakening to the call of its destiny and is scanning the new horizons with eager hope. A new spirit of earnestness, confidence and resolution is abroad in the land. In all directions are visible the stirrings of a new life. The Musalmans of India would be false to themselves and the traditions of their past, had they not shared to the full the new hope that is moving India's patriotic sons to-day, or had they failed to respond to the call of their country. Their gaze, like that of their Hindu fellow-countrymen, is fixed on the future.

But gentlemen of the All-India Moslem League, remember that the gaze of your community and of the whole country is at this moment fixed on you. The decisions that you may take in this historic Hall, and at this historic Sessions of the League, will go forth with all the force and weight that can legitimately be claimed by the chosen leaders and representatives of 70 millions of Indian Musalmans. On the nature of those decisions will depend in a large measure the fate of India's future—of India's unity and of our common ideals and aspirations for constitutional freedom. The moment for decision has arrived. The alternatives are clear and unmistakable. The choice lies in our hands.

THE WAR.

The future historian, while chronicling the cataclysms and convulsions of these times, will not fail to note the conjunction of events of boundless influence and scope that have made the fortunes of India so largely depend on the united will and effort of this generation. These events have, of course, flowed from the world-shaking crisis into which Europe was plunged in August 1914. What this dark period has meant in accumulated agony, suffering, destruction and loss to mankind, is beyond any standard of computation known to history. With the unfolding of this appalling tragedy have emerged into light, stark, elemental forces of savagery that lay behind a bright and glittering mask of "Kultur," which threaten to sweep away the very foundations of civilised life and society. The issues which are in death grips on the battle-fields of three continents, go to the roots of the principles on which the fabric of modern civilisation has been reared by the energy and toil of countless generations. Freedom, justice, right and public law are pitted against despotism, aggression, anarchy and brute force and the result of this deadly combat will decide the future of mankind—whether the end will come with a stricken and shattered world, lying bleeding and helpless under the iron heel of the tyrant, with the whole of humanity stripped bare of its hope and faith and reduced to bondage, or whether the hideous nightmare will pass away and the world, redeemed by the blood of the heroic defenders of civilisation and freedom, regain its heritage of peace and enter a period of vaster and more glorious synthesis and reconstruction.

INDIA'S LOYALTY

These are tremendous issues and the blood of every Indian with his usual gift of quick moral perception is stirred by the feeling that he is a citizen of an empire which has staked its all in a supreme endeavour to vindicate the cause of freedom and of right. What India has given in this fellowship of service and sacrifice has been a free and spontaneous tribute to the ideals of the great British nation, as well as a necessary contribution to the strength of the fighting forces of civilisation, which are so valiantly rolling back the tides of scientifically organised barbarism. In this willing service of the people of India, there has been no distinction of class or creed. It has come from every part of the land and from every community with equal readiness and devotion. In this service there has been no cold, calculating instinct at work. It has sprung from a clear, compelling sense of duty and moral sympathy and not from any commercial desire to make a safe political investment. India's loyalty to the Empire has set no price on itself.

RECONSTRUCTION.

After such colossal upheavals as this War, the world cannot quietly slip back into its old grooves of life and thought. Much of what the existing generations have known in social and political arrangements is visibly passing away under a deluge of blood and fire. The thick crust of materialism and pampered ease, the inertia of habit, the cramping weight of convention and of institutions that have outlived their use, have fallen off from the lives of the great Western Democracies under the stress of this great struggle for their existence. They have been thrown back on themselves. In the hot furnace of elemental passions, the trifles are being burnt to ashes, the gold is being made pure of dross; and when the terrible ordeal has passed, the liberated soul will feel almost primeval ease and power to plan, to build and to create afresh ampler and freer conditions of life for the future. The range of choice would be unlimited and the need for bold constructive efforts in various directions vital and urgent. Europe after the War will call for a statesmanship of a new order to undertake the gigantic tasks of peace. The greatest victory for freedom will have to be conserved. Free nations will have to learn to live freely and intensely. Freedom itself will have to be organised, its bounds made vaster and its powers of self-preservation strengthened and increased.

THE INDIAN PROBLEM.

These tasks have peculiar urgency and significance in the case of the vast and various communities comprising the British Empire. And among the complex series of problems relating to the Imperial reconstruction awaiting British statesmanship, none is of more anxious moment than the problem of reconstruction in India. I need not set about to discuss in detail the Indian problem in all its bearings. It has been discussed threadbare by all manner of men from every conceivable angle of vision. However, there are two cardinal facts about the Indian situation which practical statesmanship will have to take into account while addressing itself to the study of the problem and its adequate solution. There is, first, the great fact of the British Rule in India with its Western character and standards of administration, which, while retaining absolute power of initiative, direction and decision, has maintained for many decades unbroken peace and order in the land, administered even-handed justice, brought the Indian mind, through a widespread system of Western education, into contact with the thought and ideals of the West and thus led to the birth of a great and living movement for the intellectual and moral regeneration of the people. Here I may quote from the speech of H. E. Lord Chelmsford delivered in Calcutta the other day: "The growing self-respect and self-consciousness of her (India's) people are plants that we ourselves have watered." Secondly, there is the fact of the existence of a powerful, unifying process—the most vital and interesting result of Western education in the country—which is creating out of the diverse mass of race and creed a new India fast growing to unity of thought, purpose and outlook, responsive to new appeals of territorial patriotism and nationality, stirring with new energy and aspiration and becoming daily more purposeful and eager to recover its birth-right to direct its own affairs and govern itself. To put it briefly, we have a powerful and efficient Bureaucracy of British officers responsible only to the British Parliament, governing, with methods known as benevolent despotism, a people that have grown fully conscious of their destiny and are peacefully struggling for political freedom. This is the Indian problem in a nutshell. The task of British statesmanship is to find a prompt, peaceful, and enduring solution of this problem.

If it were possible to isolate the tangled group of social and political phenomena and subject it to a thorough investigation by reason unalloyed by sentiment, it would be infinitely easier to find a safe and sure path for Indian political development and advance. But, as you know pure unalloyed reason is not the chief motive power in human things. In the affairs of our common secular existence, we have to deal not with angels, but with men, with passions, prejudices, personal idiosyncrasies, innumerable cross-currents of motive, of desire, hope, fear and hate. The Indian problem has all such formidable complications in its texture. We have, for instance, the large and trained body of English officials who carry on the administration of the country and exercise power over the wellbeing and happiness of the teeming millions of this land. They are most of them hard-working, efficient and conscientious public servants, and yet they are beset by the prejudices and limitations that mark them as a class apart. They are naturally conservative, have a rooted horror of bold administrative changes or constitutional experiments, are reluctant to part with power or associate Indians freely in the government of the country. Their main concern appears to be to work the machine smoothly, content to go through their common round from day to day; and they feel bored and worried and upset by the loud, confident and unsettling accents of New India. All this is eminently human, but it also means an enormous aggravation of the difficulties in the path of final settlement. It means in actual experience the growth of a tremendous class-interest, the interest of the governing class as distinct from, if not wholly opposed to, the interest of the governed. It is, in fact, the existence of this vast, powerful and by no means silent "interest" that explains the origin and wide currency of certain shallow, bastard and desperate political maxims, which are flung into the face of Indian patriots at the least provocation. They are familiar enough to all students of Indian affairs As a sample, we may take the following:—

(1) Democratic institutions cannot thrive in the environment of the East. (Why? Were democratic institutions unknown to the Hindus and Mahomedans in the past? What was the village Panchayet? What are the history, the traditions, the literature and the precepts of Islam? There are no people in the world who are more democratic even in their religion than the Musalmans.)

(2) The only form of Government suitable to India is autocracy, tempered by English (European) efficiency and character. (All nations have had to go through the experience of despotic or autocratic government at one time or the other in the history of the world. Russia was liberated to a certain extent only a few years ago. France and England had to struggle before they conquered the autocracy.

Is India to remain under the heel of a novel form of autocracy in the shape of bureaucracy for all time to come, when Japan and even China have set up constitutional Governments on the democratic lines of Great Britain and America ?)

(3) (*a*) The interests of the educated classes are opposed to those of the Indian masses and

(*b*) The former would oppress the latter if the strong protecting hand of the British official were withdrawn.

(This astonishing proposition beats all reason and sense. It is suggested that we who are the very kith and kin of the masses, most of us springing from the middle classes, are likely to oppress the people if more power is conferred; that the masses require protection at the hands of the English Officials, between whom and the people there is nothing in common; that our interests are opposed to those of the masses—in what respect, it is never pointed out—and that, therefore, the monopoly of the administrative control should continue in the hands of non-Indian officials. This insidious suggestion, which is so flippantly made, is intended to secure the longest possible lease for the bureaucracy and to enjoy their monopoly. But it can neither stand the light of facts, nor the analysis of truth. One has only to look at the past records of the Congress for more than a quarter of a century and of the All-India Moslem League to dismiss this specious plea. The educated people of this country have shown greater anxiety and solicitude for the welfare and advancement of the masses than for any other question during the last quarter of a century.)

(4) Indians are unfit to govern themselves. (With this last question I propose to deal later in my speech.)

These are a few of the baseless and silly generalities in which the advocates of the existing methods of Indian governance indulge freely and provocatively when the least menace arises to the monopoly of the bureaucratic authority and power.

INTERNAL SITUATION.

Again, if we turn to the internal situation in India, we meet with a set of social, ethnological and cultural conditions unparalleled in recorded history. We have a vast continent inhabited by 315 millions of people sprung from various racial stocks, inheriting various cultures and professing a variety of religious creeds. This stupendous human group, thrown together under one physical and political environment, is still in various stages of intellectual and moral growth. All this means a great diversity of outlook, purpose and endeavour. Every Indian Nationalist who has given close and anxious thought to the problem of nation-building in India, fully realises the magnitude of his task. He is not afraid of admitting frankly that difficulties exist in his path. Such difficulties have no terrors for him. They are already vanishing before the forces which are developing in the New Spirit.

INDIA FOR THE INDIANS.

Well, these are the broad aspects of the Indian problem and they will give you a fairly general idea of the obstacles that stand in the way of a full and speedy realisation of the ideals of Indian patriots. We have a powerfully organised body of conservative "interest" on the one hand, and a lack of complete organisation of the national will and intelligence on the other. There is however, one fundamental fact, that stands out clear and unmistakable, which no sophistry of argument and no pseudo-scientific theories about colour and race can disguise. Amid the clash of warring interests and the noise of foolish catchwords, no cool-headed student of Indian affairs can lose sight of the great obvious truism that *India is in the first and the last resort for the Indians.* Be the time near or distant, the Indian people are bound to attain to their full stature as a self-governing nation. No force in the world can rob them of their destiny and thwart the purposes of Providence. British statesmanship has not become bankrupt or utterly bereft of its faculty of clear political perception; and it is, therefore, bound to recognise that the working of the law of national development in India, which came to birth with the British Rule itself, and is daily gathering momentum under the pressure of the world-forces of freedom and progress, must sooner or later produce a change in the principles and methods of Indian governance. It is inevitable. Then why fight against it, why ignore it, why should not rather there be honest, straightforward efforts to clear the way of doubts suspicions and senseless antagonisms to that glorious consummation? Leaving aside hair-brained twaddle of the tribe of scientific peddlers who love to sit in judgment on the East and ape political philosophy, no man with the least pretensions to commonsense, can affect to maintain that the Indian humanity is stamped with a ruthless psychology and cramped for ever within the prison of its skull. If the Indians are not the Pariahs of Nature, if they are not out of the pale or operation of the laws that govern mankind elsewhere, if their minds can grow in knowledge and power and can think and plan and organise together for common needs of the present and for common hopes of the future, then the only future for them is self-government *i. e.*, the attainment of the power to apply through properly organised channels, the common national will and intelligence to the needs and tasks of their national existence. The cant of unfitness must die. The laws of Nature and the doctrines of common humanity are not different in the East.

OFFICIAL ATTITUDE

It is a great relief to think that some of the responsible British statesmen have definitely pronounced in recent years that India's ambition to attain self-Government is neither a catastrophe nor a sin. Indeed, that great and sympathetic Viceroy, Lord Hardinge, whose memory will always be cherished with affection by the people of this country, for the first time recognised the legitimacy of that vital Indian aspiration. Other indications have not been wanting of late, which go to show that our national dream and purpose is gaining the stamp of even official approval. There is, however, a world of difference between a theoretical approval of an ideal and its practical application. The supreme duty of the men that lead the forces of Indian progress is to insist that India's rulers should definitely set the ideal before them as the ultimate goal to be attained within reasonable time and should accelerate the pace accordingly. All our difficulties now arise from the steady reluctance on the part of Indian officialdom to keep this end definitely in view and move faster. Mere sympathy divorced from resolute and active progressive policy can hardly ameliorate the situation. Honeyed words alone cannot suffice. We may congratulate each other about a changed "angle of vision" and yet remain where we are till doomsday. The time for definite decision and a bold move forward has arrived. The vital question to-day is :—Is India fit to be free and to what extent? There can be no shelving of the issue at this juncture. It must be settled one way or the other. If she is not fit to-day, she has got to be made fit for self-Government. This, I maintain, is no less a duty and responsibility of the Government than the people themselves.

TEST OF FITNESS.

Is India fit for freedom? We, who are present here to-day, know full well that from the Indian standpoint there can be but one answer. Our critics would probably challenge our conviction. Our only reply to them would be to go forward and put the matter to the proof. After all, what is the test of fitness? If we turn to history, we find that in the past only such people have been declared to have been fit for freedom who fought for it and attained it. We are living in different times. Peace has its victories. We are fighting and can only fight constitutional battles. This peaceful struggle is not and will not be wanting in the quality of vigour and sacrifice, and we are determined to convince the British Empire that we are fit for the place of a partner within the Empire, and nothing less will satisfy India.

MOVEMENT FOR UNITY.

But apart from the numerous other considerations that have repeatedly been urged in support of the claims of India to responsible and representative form of Government, the one that has grown to be of infinitely larger weight and urgency is the living and vigorous spirit of patriotism and national self-consciousness which is chafing under irksome restraints and is seeking wider and legitimate outlets for service and self-expression. The strength and volume of this spirit, this pent-up altruistic feeling and energy of youth, can be easily realised by those who have their finger on the pulse of the country. The most significant and hopeful aspect of this spirit is that it has taken its rise from a new-born movement in the direction of national unity which has brought Hindus and Musalmans to-gether in volving and brotherly service for the common cause. Bombay had the good fortune to see the Indian National Congress and the All-India Moslem League meet for the first time in the same city last December. These simultaneous Sessions were brought about with no little labour, anxiety and trouble. I do not wish to go into past controversy, but I venture to say that the Session of the All-India Moslem League at Bombay will go down to posterity as peculiarly interesting in its results. The so-called opponents of ours, although for the time being they caused the utmost anxiety and individual risks—which, after all, do not count in a national movement—have, I cannot help saying, rendered the greatest service to our cause. Their unjust attitude served only to stiffen the back of the community. The League rose Phoenixlike, stronger, more solidified and determined in its ideals and aspirations, with added strength of resolution in carrying out its programme. And to-day your historic City of Lucknow, the centre of Musalman culture and intellect, where three years ago the All-India Moslem League laid down our cherished ideal of self-Government under the aegis of the British Crown, is witnessing the simultaneous Sessions of the Indian National Congress and the All-India Moslem League once more. Indeed, the person who fails to read in the Hindu-Moslem rapprochment within the last few years the first great sign of the birth of united India has little knowledge of the political conditions of a few years ago and has no business to talk of India's future

IDEALS OF THE LEAGUE

I need hardly say that the Hindu-Moslem question had hitherto lain as a colossal riddle athwart the numerous unifying forces that make for the evolution of a common Indian

Nationality. The new temper that we witness to-day is the measure of the change that has happily come over Hindu-Moslem relations. What this change really signifies can only be judged by a reference to the state of things that obtained only a few years ago, when mutual distrust and suspicion were rampant and communal bigots on either side ruled the roost. Everyone of us can easily recall the frame of Moslem mind and feeling in which the All-India Moslem League was founded at Dacca. To put it frankly, the All-India Moslem League came into existence as an organisation with the main object of safeguarding Moslem interests. Musalmans, as a community, had till then abstained from all manner of political agitation and they were naturally moved by the loud and insistent demand for constitutional and administrative reforms which Hindu politicians were pressing on the Indian Government. They felt—and rightly—the need of organising themselves for political action, lest the impending changes initiated by a liberal Secretary of State should swamp them altogether as a community. This was perhaps the only course open to a community proud of the traditions of its past, yet weak in numbers and lacking the strength that organised political activity alone can give. The main principle on which the first All-India Moslem political organisation was based, was the retention of Moslem communal individuality strong and unimpaired in any constitutional readjustment that might be made in India in the course of its political evolution. The creed has grown and broadened with the growth of political life and thought in the community. In its general outlook and ideal as regards the future, the All-India Moslem League stands abreast of the Indian National Congress and is ready to participate in any patriotic efforts for the advancement of the country as a whole. In fact, this readiness of the educated Moslems, only about a decade after they first entered the field of politics, to work shoulder to shoulder with the other Indian communities for the common good of all, is to my mind the strongest proof of the value and need of the separate Moslem political organisation at present. I have been a staunch Congressman throughout my public life and have been no lover of sectarian cries, but it appears to me that the reproach of "separatism" sometimes levelled at Musalmans, is singularly inept and wide of the mark, when I see this great communal organisation rapidly growing into a powerful factor for the birth of United India. A minority must, above everything else, have a complete sense of security before its broader political sense can be evoked for co-operation and united endeavour in the national tasks. To the Musalmans of India that security can only come through adequate and effective safeguards as regards their political existence as a community. Whatever my individual opinion may be, I am here to interpret and express the sense of the overwhelming body of Moslem opinion, of which the All-India Moslem League is the political organ.

HINDU-MOSLEM RELATIONS.

It is a matter of infinite gratification to me as well as to all patriotic Musalmans that the Moslem communal position in this matter has been recognised and met in an ungrudging spirit by the leaders of the great Hindu community This was so amply demonstrated by the happy and unanimous decision that was arrived at by the Committees of the Indian National Congress and the All-India Moslem League that met at Calcutta only last November. Our joint Conferences in Lucknow were marked by honest efforts on either side to find a lasting solution of our differences, and I rejoice to think that a final settlement has at last been reached which sets the seal on Hindu-Moslem co-operation and opens a new era in the history of our country. A few irreconcilable spirits in either camp may still exist here and there, but the atmosphere has on the whole been rid of the menace of sectarian thunder and the prospects of the future are bright with a promise that gladdens the hearts of India's devoted sons. Just as I have no sympathy with a member of my community who even with an assured communal existence would not extend the hand of fellowship to his Hindu brother, so I cannot appreciate the attitude of the Hindu patriot who would insist on his pound of flesh, though, in this struggle, the entire future of the country for the sake of a small gain to one side or the other, may be marred for ever. As an instance, I would like to point out the recent unfortunate controversy that was raised in these Provinces over the passing of the Municipal Act. But surely, we are not wanting in political wisdom and sagacity. Let us remember, whether Hindus or Musalmans, that New India wants a wholly different type of public worker, of more generous spirit and ampler mould, free from the egoism of sect and the narrowness of bigotry, one who can resist the temptation to crush the weak and yet would not quail before the aggression of the strong, who can rise above the petty preoccupations of the day to the higher plane of devotion and service which alone can give to a people, faith, hope, freedom and power.

SCHEME OF REFORMS.

With the satisfactory solution of the most formidable problem that stood in the path of Indian progress towards political co-operation and unity, our constitutional battle may be said to have been half won already. The united Indian demand, based on the actual needs of the country and framed with due regard to time and circumstances, must eventually prove irresistible. It must also be recognised that those responsible for the Government of India have already shown a disposition to treat the existing grievances of the people in a broader spirit of understanding and sympathy. With the restoration of peace the Indian problem will have to be dealt with on bold and generous lines and India will have to be granted her birth-right as a free, responsible and equal member of the British Empire. How this change is to be effected and what are to be the lines of development and methods of solution, are matters that have been fully occupying the thought of Indian publicists for the past two years and authoritative schemes of re-adjustment have already been formulated and placed before the Government by the nineteen elected representatives of the Imperial Council. You are aware that a committee of the All-India Moslem League was formed last year and was authorised to draw up a scheme of reform in consultation with the Committee of the Indian National Congress. That scheme is ready and will, at this Sessions, be submitted to you for your consideration and judgment.

A NEW BILL.

After you have adopted the scheme of reforms you should see that the Congress and the League take concerted measures to have a Bill drafted by constitutional lawyers as an amending Bill to the Government of India Act which embodies the present constitution of our country. This Bill when ready should be adopted by the Indian National Congress and the All-India Moslem League and a deputation of leading and representative men from both the bodies should be appointed to, see that the Bill is introduced into the British Parliament and adopted. For that purpose we should raise as large a fund as possible to supply the sinews of war until our aim and object are fulfilled.

POSITION OF INDIA IN THE EMPIRE.

The first and the foremost question that requires to be put at rest, is that the position of India in the Empire should be defined in the most unequivocal terms. It should be made clear by the Government in an authoritative manner that self-Government is not a mere distant goal that may be attained at some future indefinite time, but that self-Government for India is the definite aim and object of the Government to be given to the people within a reasonable time. That should be the aim and object of the reconstruction and reformation of the present constitution of the Government of India and immediate steps should be taken after the War to introduce the reforms towards that end in view, both by the Government and the people.

IMPERIAL PARTNERSHIP.

Reading the signs of the times, it appears that the claims of the Overseas Dominions, such as Canada, Australia and even South Africa, *viz.*, to allow them a voice in the declaration of war and the making of peace and the Imperial Foreign policy, if they are to bear the responsibilities of the Empire, cannot well be resisted, and it might follow that an Imperial Parliament may be constructed and established, England, Scotland and

Ireland having their separate parliaments for the purpose of managing their internal and domestic affairs, such as the Dominions already have. Sir Joseph Ward, addressing the meeting of the Insurance Institute at Gresham College only last month said that "in the future reconstruction of the Empire there could not be any interference with local authority and, though an Imperial Parliament was a long way off, they might now work for some effective Imperial Council and that before an organic Parliament was possible, there must be devolution in Britain to pave the way for a federal legislature overseas. The Dominions had no right even to a minority voice as to whether the nation should go to war or what the peace terms should be." He quoted Mr. Asquith's speech at the 1911 Imperial Conference in which the Prime Minister stated that "an Imperial Parliament scheme would impair the authority of the British Parliament." "Since then," Sir Joseph said, "there had been a great evolution of opinion on the subject. Mr. Bonar Law had declared as a result of the war the time was coming when the overseas Dominions would share in the Government of the Empire with Britain. He hoped that before the War ended some *modus vivendi* would be established." In the political reconstruction India, the largest part of the Empire, cannot possibly be allowed to continue a dependency, as an adjunct to England, Scotland or Ireland or to be ruled and governed by the Dominions. Hitherto the responsibility, the control and the supervision of India has been vested in Great Britain. The question naturally arises what will be the position of India if an Imperial Parliament with full representation of the Dominions is constituted? Is India to have new and additional masters? Is India to be ruled jointly by England, Scotland, Ireland and the Dominions? Are we to be handed over to this Imperial Parliament and to be thus ruled and to be governed by the Colonies? Are we not to have a status or *locus standi* in this Imperial Parliament? I feel sure that I am expressing the opinion of the entire educated people of this country that India will never allow herself to be relegated to such an intolerable position. Indeed, she does not want a change of masters, nor additional masters. If an Imperial Parliament, such as indicated above, is established, India's right should be recognised and her voice in that Imperial Parliament must be fully and properly secured and represented by her own sons in the Councils of the Empire.

MINIMUM DEMANDS.

Next, it is well-known that the reforms that are sought by the people of India to be introduced in the constitutional Government of India, were fully adumbrated recently by the 19 elected members of the Imperial Legislative Council and I do not wish to repeat them here, as I believe you are all familiar with them already. I was one of the signatories and I would urge upon you to follow them substantially so far as fundamental principles are involved in those proposals. Those demands were formulated by responsible men who owe duty to the Government and the people alike as "chosen representatives" not in a spirit of bargaining. Those demands are the minimum in the strictest sense of the word. It is said that these are extravagant demands. It is said it is a big thing. It is said that we are not yet ready for them. It is said that if these reforms are introduced, there will be chaos, and particularly the Anglo-Indian Press is not only most unreasonable and disappointing, but alarmed. These are mere destructive methods. Similar fears were raised and arguments advanced when the Minto-Morely Reforms were on the Legislative anvil. But what is the verdict now, official and non-official, after nearly seven years of actual trial? Need I give the answer? We have not been favoured either by our critics or by the Government as to what is the alternative scheme. We are not taken into the confidence of the secret chambers of the Government where the Goverument of India, it is said, have been deliberating upon and preparing a despatch containing their proposals of reform to be submitted to the Secretary of State for India. In England, the representatives of the Colonies and the Press and the people and the Ministers are freely discussing the reconstruction of the constitution of the Empire after the War, may even before the War is over it is suggested to set up an Imperial Council, whereas in India we are denied the opportunity of knowing even what the Government are contemplating. It will be a great misfortune if any decisions are arrived at with regard to the future of India by the Government and the Secretary of State for India without the proposals being published and placed before the country at large for public criticism and opinion. I must earnestly urge upon the Government that before any final decision is arrived at, the proposed reforms should be published and the people should be given an opportunity to urge their views, and that they should be taken into their confidence. I feel that if the people are bitterly disappointed at this juncture, it will mean the greatest disaster to the future progress of this country.

QUESTION OF THE CALIPHATE.

I should be failing in my duty towards my own people and the Government if I did not, at this crisis, make it clear that of the many delicate questions, there is none that requires a closer attention and study than the question of the Caliphate by the Government and the Ministers of Great Britain. The sentiments and feelings and the religious convictions not only of the Musalmans of India but of the Musalmans of the world are not to be lightly treated. The loyalty of the Musalmans of India to the Government is no small asset. From the very commencement of the great crisis through which the British Empire has been passing, the allegiance of the Musalmans to the Crown and their loyalty to the Government has remained whole-hearted and unshaken. May I, therefore, urge that the Government should have regard for their dearest and most sacred religious feelings and under no circumstances interfere with the question of the future of the Caliphate. It should be left entirely to the Musalmans to acknowledge and accept their own Caliph. I do not desire to dilate on this grave and delicate subject; but much deeper currents underly this exceptional exhortation of mine, which I have ventured to make both in the interests of the Musalmans and the Government of Great Britain, than it would be expedient at present to discuss on a public platform. But the Musalmans may well claim that their feelings and sentiments relating to their most cherished traditions should receive consideration in the general policy of the Empire, particularly when they coincide with the demands of justice, humanity and international obligations

HOLY PLACES OF ISLAM.

As a spokesman of the Musalmans of India, I must here acknowledge that the noble assurance of the British Government given to them through H. E. Lord Hardinge, the late Viceroy of India, as regards the Holy Places of Islam, was received by them not only with the utmost satisfaction, but with profound gratitude.

MOSLEM ATTITUDE.

I may say a word as to the attitude of the Musalmans of India towards the Government. Our clear duty is to be loyal and respectful, without stooping to a cringing policy. We want no favours, and crave for no partial treatment. That is demoralizing to the community and injurious to the State. The Musalmans must learn to have self respect what we want is a healthy and fair impetus to be given to our aspirations and ideals as a community and it is the most sacred duty of Government to respond to that claim. Towards the Hindus our attitude should be of good-will and brotherly feelings. Co-operation in the cause of our Motherland should be our guiding principle. India's real progress can only be achieved by a true understanding and harmonious relations between the two great sister communities. With regard to our own affairs, we can depend upon nobody but ourselves. We should infuse greater spirit of solidarity into our society. We should remove the root causes and the evil effects of the process of disintegration. We should maintain a sustained loyalty to and co-operation with each other. We should sink personal differences and subordinate personal ambitions to the well-being of the community. We must recognise that no useful purpose is served in petty disputes and in forming party combinations. We should not lose the sympathy of our well-wishers in India and in England by creating a wrong impression that we, as a community, are out only for self-interest and self-gain. We must show by our words and deeds that we sincerely and earnestly desire a healthy National unity. For the rest, the 70 millions of Musalmans need not fear.

RELIGIOUS DIFFERENCE.

A few days ago I came across a paragraph in the "Bombay Chronicle," the well-known daily paper of Bombay, with its Editor Mr. B. G. Horniman, a friend of the Musalmans who has rendered great services to us. It is as follows :—

"The following incident, reported by the *Amrita Bazaar Patrika*, may well be read with profit by those whose perverse imaginations, in spite of proofs to the contrary, always see in the differences of religions in India an irremoveable bar against placing Indians in high offices of trust and responsibility :—

This is how H. H. the Nizam has just disposed of a Hindu-Musalman dispute in his territory. Well, for about a year or so, there sprang a quarrel between the Hindus and the Musalmans of Warrangal about the building of a mosque in a prominent Hindu locality. In spite of many protests from the Hindu population, the other party persisted on constructing one The Hindus then appealed to His Highness with the result that he was pleased to appoint a committee of enquiry consisting of two Musalmans and one Hindu to report on the matter The report was in favour of the Hindus and His Highness has been pleased to pass his orders accordingly"

"The action taken by H. H. the Nizam, it need hardly be added, was in accordance with the traditional policy always adopted by the rulers of Hyderabad."

Why can't we in British India, the Hindus and the Musalmans, try the methods which prove so successful in the territories of H. H. the Nizam, to settle our differences?

CONCLUSION.

In conclusion I cannot do better than quote a passage from the recent speech of the Prime Minister Mr. Lloyd George, every word of which almost literally applies to the conditions in India. Referring to the Irish situation he said :—

"He was convinced now that it was a misunderstanding, partly racial, partly religious. It was to the interest of both to have it removed. But there seemed to have been some evil chance that frustrated every effort made for the achievement of better relations. He had tried once but did not succeed. But the fault was not entirely on one side. He had felt the whole time that we were moving in an atmosphere of nervous suspicious and distrust, pervasive and universal of everything and everybody. He was drenched with suspicion of Irishmen by Englishmen and of Englishmen by Irishmen and, worse and most fatal of all, by the suspicion of Irishmen of Irishmen. It was a quagmire of distrust which clogged the footsteps of progress. That was the real enemy of Ireland. If that could be slain, he believed, it would accomplish an act of reconciliation that would make Ireland greater and Britain greater and would make the United Kingdom and the Empire greater than they ever were before.

The Renaissance of India really lies in our own hands. Let us work and trust to God, so that we may leave a richer heritage to our children than all the gold of the world, *viz.*, Freedom for which no sacrifice is too great.

BOMBAY PROVINCIAL CONFERENCE, 1916.

In presiding over the sixteenth Bombay Provincial conference held at Ahmedabad in October 1916, the Hon'ble Mr. Jinnah delivered the following address:—

BROTHER DELEGATES, LADIES AND GENTLEMEN.

I need hardly say that in calling me to preside over the deliberations of the 16th Bombay Provincial Conference, you have conferred upon me the greatest honour that is within the gift of the people of this Presidency. I do not know why your choice has fallen upon me, but when the call came, I considered it my duty as a servant of the cause, to obey it and I am here to-day amongst you. I most sincerely thank you for the honourable position to which you have raised me to-day and I shall try to do my duty as a President and I have no doubt that I shall have your entire support and co-operation in carrying out those duties during our deliberation.

This is the first time after many years since the unfortunate differences arose in Surat, that the United Provincial Conference has met and the responsibility—the peculiar responsibility—therefore, rests on me and all of you correctly to voice the public opinion of the country and the Presidency.

Since the last meeting of the Provincial Conference at Poona we have—nay, the Empire has—lost one of its greatest soldiers, Lord Kitchener and in Sir Pherozeshah Mehta one of its greatest politicians and statesman.

We deeply mourn the great loss of such men especially at this juncture of stress and great crisis through which India and the whole Empire is passing.

In Sir Chimunbhai Madhavlal to our great sorrow we have lost a captain of Industry and Commerce for which Ahmedabad is so famous. He was a great philanthrophist and patron of learning and education.

In Mr. Daji Abaji Khare, I say with the deepest sorrow, we have lost a man of sturdy independence and a quiet, but devoted worker for the cause of India. He rendered great and continuous valuable services to the Indian National Congress from its early days of storm and difficulties.

In Mr. Govindrao Appaji Patel, I regret to say we have lost a zealous and devoted worker in the public cause in the Province of Gujarat. May the soul of these great and devoted men who worked for the Empire and public cause rest in peace. And let us pray that we may soon have other such servants who may take their places and keep up their great traditions and follow their noble examples and maintain the prestige and a great name of this mighty Empire.

Two questions above all are uppermost in our thoughts and are engrossing our mind at the present moment. The War and what is going to happen after the successful termination of this titanic struggle that has overshadowed the entire civilized world. India has stood faithful and loyal to the British Empire from the very commencement; she has poured out her treasure and shed the blood of some of her noblest sons on the battlefields of Flanders, Africa, Egypt and Mesopotamia for the defence of the Empire. It may be said once for all that the people of India are proud to be a part of the British Empire and that their loyalty is as true and firm as that of any other Britisher in any part of the Empire, not excluding Great Britain and there is no doubt that India will to the end stand faithfully by the British Empire But she wishes no longer to continue as the subject race, or to put in the words of Lord Hardinge "the trusty dependent," but claims to be an equal partner with the other members of the Empire.

It is a matter of great rejoicing that the enemy has failed in his efforts at Verdun. The gallant and noble defence of Verdun by the French people has won the admiration of the world: with this signal failure on the part of the enemy, the advent of Roumania and the mighty army that England has raised with ample munition, has enabled the Allies successfully to take the offensive in the West. The initiative is no longer with the enemy and the tide has turned, and let us hope that it will not be long before the arms of the Allies are finally successful, and this great war ends in complete defeat of the brutal and aggressive Prussian Militarism.

We have met here to-day to consider the position of our country and the Province. There are many questions and problems which require our most earnest and serious consideration. We have met to discuss those questions and exchange our views regarding those problems. Naturally on taking a general survey of the situation, one has to face the questions :—What progress have we made within the past, half a century? What is our present position? What is to be our future? What steps should be taken to remove the difficulties in our way? What measures should be adopted to further the progress of our country and to attain as soon as possible our most cherished goals, namely, Self-Government under the "ægis" of the British Crown and the Provincial Autonomy foreshadowed in the Delhi Despatch of Government of India dated 25th August, 1911? It is said that there is peace and security in the country. It is said there is prosperity in the country, although two of the greatest sons of India—Mr. Dadabhoy Naoroji and Mr. Romesh Chandra Dutt—the latter with his great administrative experience of India —do not agree with the statement that there is real prosperity in the country, it is said that the administration of the conntry is most efficient and the Collectors and the Commissioners are devoted to their duties and to the Districts where they work and that they have the interests and the welfare of the Ryots at their heart; it is said that the British Soldiers and British Navy are protecting our lives and property, our hearths and homes are quite secure and safe. It is said that all is going well—everything is managed properly on behalf of the people by the Civil Service. Assuming all this to be correct and granting that there is peace, prosperity and efficient administration entirely in the hands of the Civil Servants, is that any reason that the control, the management and the administration of the affairs of our country should for ever be continued as a monopoly in the hand of a bureaucratic Government? Is it any argument to say that since the Bureaucracy have under certain conditions managed the affairs of the country well for half a century and more, that therefore they should be given a permanent monopoly—no matter what the changed conditions are and how much those conditions may have altered? Is that any reason why the Commissioned ranks in the Military and Naval Services should be closed to the sons of India? Is that any reason for denying to Indians the right to join the Volunteer Corps and for continuing the application of the Arms Act?

PARLIAMENT AND INDIA.

The first question that arises is, whether this system of administration conducted by the Civil Servants, who are neither under the control of or responsible to the people who pay their salaries can any longer continue. It is said that they are responsible to the Secretary of State for India and that the Secretary of State for India in his turn is responsible to Parliament. I will only quote from one of the leading Journals in England, the "Manchester Guardian" what appeared in its columns recently with regard to the responsibility of Parliament in matters affecting India :—

"A new Viceroy and a new Secretary of State are in office. From the date of Lord Morley's translation seven years ago to that of Mr. Austen Chamberlain's acceptance of the India Office last summer, Indian questions in the commons have been dealt with by the Under-Secretary; and it is surely an anomaly and sometimes of a scandal that not once since his appointment, has the house had an opportunity of hearing from Mr. Chamberlain a full statement upon the condition of India or an exposition of his policy. And yet as the whole Empire realises, the position of India in the Imperial system is deeply affected by the movement of events as it will be by every measure of after-War policy that may be decided by England and her Allies. Moreover the internal life of India to-day is undergoing changes more rapid than any hitherto known and the Government by deciding upon the publication of the Royal Commission's Report on the Public Services, has acknowledged the wisdom and necessity of discussion upon proposals for administrative reform. It is high time that Parliament began to take the affairs of India seriously and that the official myth that India wants nothing but to be let alone were exploded. If Parliament is to ignore the vast responsibility of the Government of this mighty dependency, what is the use of a Parliament which calls itself Imperial?"

Ladies and gentlemen, is it not an anomaly that the domestic affairs of a country with a population of three hundred millions and more should practically be under the control and the management of (as it is often said by ministers and writers) an alien bureaucracy, not responsible to the people of the country, under no control of the people who pay taxation, but only accountable to the Secretary of State for India, who himself has never been to India, and his Council, which again is composed mostly of retired Civil Servants, sitting seven thousand miles away from India; and the Secretary of State again in his turn theoretically responsible to Parliament for his stewardship, though in practice, hardly ever is his stewardship called to account or critically investigated by Parliament? Lord Courtney deprecated the position of the Secretary of State for India in the following words:—

"The Secretary of State is a member of the Cabinet, which must possess the confidence of the House of Commons. In the end, the National Will must have its way here as elsewhere; but checks and obstacles are interposed which, perhaps, insensibly moderates its force. No part of the expense involved in the Government of India comes before the House of Commons in Committee Supply. The salary of the Colonial Secretary is voted by Parliament and there is thus a possibility of annually reviewing his policy in the full activity of the Parliamentary Sessions. The salary of the Indian Secretary of State is paid by India and never comes before the House of Commons. At the end of the Session, generally after the Appropriation Bill is read a second time, the Indian Budget is submitted, and this consists of the review of the financial situation in India, followed by, after a desultory discussion, a resolution simply affirming that the Indian accounts show certain totals of Income and Expenditure; it may be doubted whether this does not betray too great a jealousy of the House of Commons. If the salary of the Indian Secretary of State were submitted like the Colonial Secretary's to a vote, the opportunity for a real debate would be given, which experience suggests, would be used rather than abused."

But I go further: Is it possible or natural as a rule for members of Parliament to grasp or grapple with questions affecting the internal administration and progress of India? When it was founded that that was not possible in the case of Australia, Canada and South Africa, with few millions of population, would it not be miraculous if they continued to manage successfully the affairs of India by Parliament sitting in London? Having regard to the rapidly growing wants and demands of the people and the tremendous progress and changes that India is going through every few years, is it possible to govern India from Whitehall or Downing Street? To those who know India and understand India, it is clear that she no longer will merely obey, but wants to manage her own affairs. Peace, prosperity and security which satisfied her a decade ago are no longer enough. The Soul of Young India has been roused and it yearns for Political Freedom. However well our physical and material wants may be provided for, that is not sufficient. India wants to raise herself to a status which will command the respect of the Nations of the world for her and which will be befitting her National honour and self-respect. It is not now a question of a few posts; it is no longer a question of a few grievances or reform of internal matters of administration; it is a question of complete change of policy. The question at issue is not merely of details but it relates to the fundamental structure of the Government and we require a statesman to deal with the present situation and refashion and reconstruct the constitution of the Government of India. It is said that there is dissatisfaction in the Country;

it is said a political agitation is kept up which is embarrassing to the Government; it is said that the Home Rule League movement is not desirable; but what is the cause of it all? Surely, those are not merely the signs of an excessive imagination as explained by some people for want of better knowledge. It is quite clear that this is due to the awakened political consciousness of the people, who demand a new polity and resent—and rightly resent—the differential treatment which is meted out to them socially, commercially and politically. It is a mistake to construe this resentment as a mark of disloyalty. It will be wisdom to root out the fundamental causes of dissatisfaction and discontent.

A NEW SPIRIT.

A new spirit is abroad. It is young India, who, to put it in the words of Lord Morley, "leave our Universities intoxicated with the ideas of freedom, nationality and self-Government," have to be satisfied. It will be cold comfort to them to say that free institutions are the special privilege of the West. In order to meet the present situation, in my humble opinion, the Members of the Indian Civil Service must now realise that, as the Government of India from autocracy was transferred to bureaucracy, so the time has come when from bureaucracy it must tend towards democracy. They have wielded the sceptre of supreme control for a long time and their dominion in India has not been without its benefits to the Country. But the time has come, when, however unwilling —and naturally unwilling—they must part with their supreme control and dominion. Amongst the many benefits that have been conferred upon India by British Rule, perhaps the greatest of boons, albeit, an indirect one which India has received at the hands of the English people, has been the birth of a genuine spirit of patriotism. To put it in the words of a member of the Civil Service, who has given much thought to the problem of bureaucratic Government, "it is the patriotism which seeks its ideals, not in military glory or the apotheosis of a king, but in the advancement of the people. Informed by this spirit and strong in the material benefits flowing from British Rule, India now knocks at the portal of democracy. Bureaucracy has served its purpose. Though the Indian Civil Service were manned by angels from heaven, the incurable defects of a bureaucratic Government must pervert their best intentions and make them foes of political progress. It must now stand aside and in the interest of the country it has served so long and so truly, make over the dominion to other hands not in dishonour, but in honour, proudly as ship-builders who deliver to seamen the completed ship, may they now yield up the direction of India." This will require self-abnegation, self-sacrifice—not for their own nation but for India, for humanity. It will require sympathy and understanding such as no nation has ever felt for a foreign people. Will the Civil Service rise to this supreme duty that they owe to the three hundred millions of people of this Country? Let me quote the words of His Excellency Lord Hardinge from his speech at the United Service Club which he addressed to a large number of representative officials, he said :—

"England has instilled into this Country the culture and civilization of the West with all its ideals of liberty and self-respect. It is not enough for her now to consider only the material outlook of India. It is necessary for Her to cherish the aspirations of which She has herself sown the seed and English Officials are gradually awakening to the fact that high as were the aims and remarkable the achievements of their predecessors, a still nobler task lies before them in the present and the future guiding the uncertain and faltering steps of Indian development along sure and safe paths. The new role of guide, philosopher and friend is opening before you and it is worthy of your greatest efforts. It requires in you gifts of imagination and sympathy and imposes upon you self-sacrifice, for it means that slowly, but surely you must divest yourselves of some of the powers you have hitherto wielded."

It is universally recognised that if you deprive a nation of all share in its own Government, in the forging of its destiny, you emasculate its energies, undermine its character and sear, as if with a hot iron, its self-respect. In the sphere of intellect such a Government spells not progress, but decay.

PROVINCIAL GOVERNMENT.

This now brings me to the question as to what should be done. This being a Provincial Conference, I will now confine myself only to the Provincial Government. The first principle that is to be observed is the principle of devolution and decentralization. But this, as I understand, implies that the ultimate control of the Imperial authority in Legislative as well as in Executive matters, is kept intact and in reserve to be used whenever necessary. And a better illustration of this principle cannot be found than in the Home Rule Bill which was passed by the House of Commons conferring self-Government on Ireland. Prof. Morgan in an authoritative exposition of the New Irish Constitution points out that "the Bill is quite outside the category of Federalism in that, while it proposes a delegation of authority both in Legislative and Executive, there is none of the distribution of Sovereignty which is a distinguishing characteristic of a Federation. The Executive power in Ireland will continue vested in His Majesty. The Legislative authority will be subject to an Imperial veto and to the supremacy of the Imperial Parliament with its powers of concurrent Legislation and the Irish Courts will be subject to the Appellate Jurisdiction of an Imperial Court." In other words the Imperial power will be supreme in the Executive, the Legislative and the Judicial sphere. The position of the Executive and Legislative authorities in India is quite similar and although the element of self-Government in every one of them is more or less non-existent, the legal relation between the Imperial and Provincial Government is based on the same principle. The Provincial Council is supposed to have a non-official majority. The non-official representatives are divided into elected members, nominated members, that is to say, nominated by Government and European representatives. In measures affecting the people in which Europeans are not directly concerned, they support the Government. Nominated members, being nominees of Government, are naturally inclined to take the side of Government. Past experience has shown that this has actually happened on various occasions. The non-official majority, therefore, in the Provincial Council is illusory and gives no real power to the representatives of the people. The Provincial Council at the present moment is nothing but an advisory body without possessing any power or effective control over the Government. The people or their representatives are as little associated with the real Government of the Province as they were before the Reforms of 1909 except for the introduction of one Indian member in the Executive Council of His Excellency the Governor, where again the nomination rests entirely with the Government, the people having no voice in the selection of the Indian member. The object, which the Government had in view in introducing the Reforms of 1909, as expressed by the Prime Minister in his speech in the House of Commons on the second reading of the India Council Bill, (April 1st, 1909), "that it was desirable in the circumstances to give to people of India a feeling that these Legislative Councils are not mere automatons the wires of which are pulled by the official hierarchy," it is quite clear, has not been attained.

FORM OF ADMINISTRATION.

In order to give the people of the Provincial the real and effective voice in the Government of the Province for which they are ripe the following brief outline may be indicated as to the form of administration that should be set up in our Province :—

1. The Province should have a Governor appointed from England at the head of the administration.

2. A Cabinet or Executive Council of six members, three of whom should be Indians, with the following portfolios :—

(*a*) Provincial (including Law and Justice similar to Home member).

(*b*) Finance.

(*c*) Agriculture, Irrigation and Public Works.

(*d*) Education.

(*e*) Local Government (including Sanitation and Medical Relief.)

(*f*) Industries and Commerce.

While Members of the Indian Civil Service should still be eligible for appointment to the Executive Council, no places in the Council should be reserved for them as at present under the Statute, which makes it obligatory that a certain number of the Members of the Executive Council should be appointed from Public Services.

The best men available should be appointed, whether English or Indian.

3. A substantial majority in the Council should be of elected members returned by different constituencies and interests. Mahomedans and Hindus, wherever they are in a minority, should have proper, adequate and effective representation, having regard to their numerical strength and position. There should be no nominated non-official member except as experts.

4. The Council should have the power to pass all Provincial Legislation and determine

Provincial taxation. All Resolutions in connection with the Budget as also on questions of general administration should take effect unless vetoed by the Government. More frequent meetings and longer continuous sittings will also have to be provided for. But the members of the Executive Government shall not depend individually or collectively on the support of a majority of the Council or for holding their offices. The Provincial Government, reconstituted and working under the control of the Legislative Council, should have complete charge of the internal administration of the Province. It should have independent financial powers and the present financial relationship between the Provincial Government and the Government of India should be largely revised or if necessary reversed. The Provincial Government should be required to make an annual contribution to the Government of India, fixed for a definite period. Subject to this arrangement the Imperial and Provincial Government should develop their separate system of finance, the Provincial Government being given powers of taxation and borrowing within certain limits.

No scheme of Provincial autonomy can be complete without the corresponding changes of a liberalising character being introduced into the District and Municipal administration.

It is always a difficult task to lay down any cut and dried scheme in a Presidential address, but here again I shall venture to make a few suggestions affecting the fundamental principles that underlie local self-Government in India and here I would quote from no less an authority than Lord Morley's Reform Despatch dated 27th November, 1909. It says.—"The principles that should inspire and regulate measures with this aim, can hardly be laid down on sounder and clearer terms than in the Resolution published by the Government of India on the 18th of May, 1882. I do not know where to look for a better expression of the views that should govern our policy under this important head."

This Resolution although passed as far back as 1882 by the Government of that renowned

Viceroy Lord Ripon has not still been carried out fully or given real effect to.

The first and foremost change that is necessary to be introduced in the various bodies, is that they should be wholly elected, the Provincial Government alone reserving to itself and exercising powers of control; that the present official control exercised by the Collectors and Commissioners should be removed; that the Chairman should be elected by the Boards and the ex-officio President should be done away with; that a portion of Excise revenue or some other definite source of revenue should be made over to these Bodies so that they may have adequate resources at their disposal for the due performance of their duties.

To quote again from Lord Morley's Reform Despatch, this is what he says:—

"I will venture to quote some passages in this memorable deliverance. Explaining the proposal for Local self-Government of that date, the Government of India place themselves on ground which may well be our ground also. It is not primarily, they say, 'with a view to improvement in administration that this measure is put forward and supported, it is chiefly desirable as an instrument of political and popular education,' and again, 'there appears to be great force in the argument that so long as the chief Executive officers are, as a matter of course, Chairmen of the Municipal and District Committees, there is little chance of these committees affording any effective training to their members taking any real interest in local business. The non-official members must be led to feel that real power is placed in their hands and that they have real responsibilities to discharge.' This anticipation has been, to some extent, warranted by experience. Funds have not existed for an efficient Executive staff. The official element within the local Bodies has been in many places predominant. Non-official members have not been induced to such an extent as was hoped, to take a real interest in local business because their powers and their responsibilities were not real. If Local self-Government has so far been no marked success as a training ground, it is mainly for the reason that the constitution of the local Bodies departed from what was affirmed in the Resolution to be 'the true principle' that 'the control should be exercised from without rather than from within; the Government should revise and check the acts of Local Bodies but not dictate them.' I have no doubt that the Government of India to-day will affirm and actively shape their policy upon the principle authoritatively set forth by their predecessors in 1882:—'It would be hopeless to expect any real development of self-Government if the local Bodies were subject to check and interference in matters of detail, and the respective powers of Government and of the various local Bodies should be clearly and distinctly defined by Statute so that there may be as little risk of friction and misunderstanding as possible within the limits to be laid down in each case. However the Governor-General in Council is anxious that the fullest possible liberty of action should be given to local Bodies.' "

I have made a few general observations and dealt with the Provincial Government and the question of Local self-Government. There are many other questions and important questions which I see are placed on the agenda in the form of Resolutions and I have no doubt that the speakers in charge of those Resolutions will adequately deal with them. But I cannot conclude my address without referring at least to some of the burning questions, and amongst them the most important question is the question of admission of the Indians to Commissioned ranks of the Army and Navy, the removal of the most irritating and humiliating disabilities created by statutes which have raised a bar against the people of India in joining Volunteer Corps, no matter what their rank or position in life may be; the unjust application of the Arms Act to the people of India from which the Europeans are exempted. The Press Act and its arbitrary provisions and still more its arbitrary enforcement by the Executive which is subject to no judicial check, so far as the decisions of the High Courts at the present moment go; the Defence of India Act, which was purely a War measure and to which the representatives of the people of India assented when it came before the

Imperial Council, is worked in a manner in some cases which is highly undesirable; the undue and unjustifiable delay in making elementary education free and compulsory in the selected areas is the cause of the greatest dissatisfaction and disappointment to the people.

INDIANS AND THE ARMY AND NAVY.

Now to take the question of the Army and the Navy, the only two arguments which have hitherto been advanced are that the people of the country are not fit except some sects or tribes who have followed the profession of arms as a hereditary profession. Now, first of all, is that a correct hypothesis? At the outbreak of the War, the Princes and the people of India of all classes and sections, with one voice, volunteered to support the Empire with their money and blood. Young students in England belonging to different classes of people in India, from all parts of India studying at their Universities, volunteered to enlist themselves as Territorials. For an answer, they were told that being Indians, their services could not be accepted. Then they made representations to the Secretary of State for India expressing their indignation at this differential treatment, it was said that the whole military question affecting India will be considered after the War. In Bengal a movement was started in which Sir S. P. Sinha took a leading part to start a Volunteer Corps, a large sum of money was collected and six hundred young men belonging to respectable families enlisted themselves ready to go to the Front, to fight the battle of the Empire. But they were told that that cannot be. Does the profession of a soldier require more brains, greater capacity, ingenuity than that of a lawyer, a doctor, or a poet or a scientist? If Indians are good enough to fight as Sepoys and Privates, why are they not good enough to occupy the position of officers? There cannot be a better answer than what the Indian soldiers have achieved in this War. Several of them are the proud possessors of the Victoria Cross, which, to a soldier, is the greatest honour and decoration that can be conferred upon him by the King-Emperor.

The second argument is that an army with a preponderance of the Indian element may be turned against the British Government and here I cannot but quote a more complete answer than what was given by the President of the Indian National Congress, Sir S.P. Sinha. He said: "I venture to submit in reply that anarchists and seditionists may succeed in winning over an ignorant and mercenary army, but they will never succeed in winning over a truly national army, drawn from a people made increasingly loyal by the spread of education and liberal self-governing institutions. The opening of a military career will fire the imagination and stimulate the virility of India in a way that nothing else can do. And is it too much for India to expect to be treated in the same way as Russia treats her subject races—especially after the proof India has given of the prowess of her sons and their devotion and loyalty to the Imperial Standard?"

These arguments equally apply to the Navy, where the sons of India cannot aspire to a higher position than that of Lascar in the Mercantile Marine. The time is not far distant when perhaps India will have to consider what fleet she should raise primarily for Indian Defences and as a contribution to the Imperial Navy.

The Press Act was a most unwelcome measure from its very inception. It has been characterised as a serious menace to the freedom of the Press in India; but the harsh manner in which it is enforced has roused the strongest opposition and created great discontent. The safeguards provided by the Act have proved illusory and incapable of being enforced as declared by the High Court of Calcutta. It is high time that the Government appointed a Committee of official and non-official members to consider its working since 1910 and recommend what course should be adopted to allay the just public resentment and discontent with regard to this measure,

DEFENCE OF INDIA ACT

The Defence of India Act as a War measure was accepted by the country. But its working has proved that it is a dangerous weapon placed in the hands of the Executive on whom there is no judicial check of any kind whatsoever. It would be wise to follow the procedure adopted in England to have a Committee who should have the power of revising the orders of the Executive Officers and such a committee should have an equal number of Indian members.

I have the honour and privilege of knowing His Excellency the Governor. If I may say so, Lord Willingdon is all kindness and courtesy. I hope, I am not giving out any secrets, when I say that I personally know that he is in full sympathy with our ideals and aspirations and has done much to support them. But I cannot help saying that it was a matter of profound regret that the Bombay Government of which he is the head, should have thought proper to apply the Defence of India Act, to that great English lady Mrs. Besant. Whether we agree with her or not, whether we see eye to eye with her or not on certain questions, I believe I am expressing the universal feeling of this Presidency and for the matter of that, the whole country at large, that the Order of the local Government prohibiting

Mrs. Besant to enter our Province was received with the utmost sorrow and shock. It is a grave reflection on the fair name of this Presidency and I feel it is calculated to do great harm to the dignity and the prestige of the Government itself.

With regard to elementary education being made free and compulsory, so much has been said that at this juncture I do not wish to enter into details; but the renaissance of India can only be achieved truly by a true and real foundation to be laid for self-government ultimately based on a proper system of education of national character, which in course of time would produce more and more men worthy of managing the affairs of our own country. I may have occasion at a not very distant future, when I should perhaps like to deal with this important question in detail.

THE EDUCATED CLASSES.

Before I leave this subject, I may point out that it is often put forward as a favourite argument that India is not fit for self-government because the educated classes are as yet a very small fraction in the country. In the first instance the Government, although they have recently bestirred themselves in the cause of education, have never seriously and earnestly grappled with the problem of Elementary or Primary education in India. The question have always been shelved on one ground or the other, such as want of funds, want of school buildings, want of trained teachers. On the other hand, we are told that we have not got a sufficient number of educated people. Who is responsible for it after 100 years of British Rule? But the test of the fitness of the people for self-government is not that every man, woman and child should be first educated and the hollowness of this plea was ably exposed by the late Mr. George Yule in his address as President of our National Congress in 1888. "Quoting Prof. Thorold Rogers, he pointed out that a hundred years ago, not one man in ten or one woman in twenty knew how to read or write in England. Going another century or two back, he added, the people of England, man and boy, high and low with the exception of a mere handful were steeped in gross ignorance and yet there was a House of Commons." And I believe, we have now at the present moment in India twenty millions who can read and write.

HINDUS AND MAHOMEDANS.

Now I come to the all-absorbing question which stirred India because of the declaration of the "Entente Cordiale" between the Hindus and the Mahomedans made in the City of Bombay last Christmas. I believe all thinking men are thoroughly convinced that the key-note of our real progress lies in the good-will, concord, harmony and co-operation between the two great sister communities. The true focus of progress is centred in their union and remember this is a matter which is entirely in our own hands. It was three years ago that the All-India Moslem League adopted the ideal of Self-Government under the "ægis" of the British Crown which was hailed by the Indian National Congress at Karachi where the following Resolution was passed :—

"That this Congress places on record its warm appreciation of the adoption by the

All-India Moslem League of the ideal of Self-Government for India within the British Empire and expresses its complete accord with the belief that the League has so emphatically declared at its last session that the political future of the country depends on the harmonious working and co-operation of the various communities in the country which has been the cherished ideal of the Congress. This Congress most heartily welcomes the hope expressed by the League that the leaders of the different communities will make every endeavour to find a *modus operandi* for joint and concerted action on all questions of national good and earnestly appeals to all the sections of the people to help the object which we all have at heart."

Since then the programme of the All-India Moslem League has been more and more approximated to that of the Indian National Congress. There is but one question besides the question of cow-killing and street-music which has proved not only a thorny question but an obstacle which has kept the two communities hitherto apart. But the solution is not difficult. It requires a true spirit of conciliation and give and take. The Mahomedans want proper, adequate and effective representation in the Council Chambers of the country and in the District and Municipal Boards, a claim which no right-minded Hindu disputes for a moment. But the Mahomedans further require that representation in the various boards and Council Chambers should be secured to them by means of *separate electorates.* This question of separate electorates from the top to bottom has been before the country ever since 1909 and rightly or wrongly the Mussalman community is absolutely determined for the present to insist upon separate electorates. To most of us the question is no more open to further discussion or argument as it has become a mandate of the community. As far as I understand, the demand for separate electorates is not a matter of policy but a matter of necessity to the Mahomedans who require to be roused from the coma and torpor into which they had fallen so long. I would therefore appeal to my Hindu Brethren that in the present state of position they should try to win the confidence and trust of the Mahomedans who are, after all, in the minority in the country. If they are determined to have separate electorates, no resistance should be shown to their demand.

There are other questions of most vital and paramount importance to both the Hindus and Mahomedans, that require united and concerted action. Differences in details such as, method of securing to Mahomedans, their adequate share in the Council Chambers, Municipal and District Boards should not be allowed to create an "impasse" and one side or the other must give in. I would, therefore, appeal to my Hindu friends to be generous and liberal and welcome and encourage other activities of Mahomedans even if it involves some sacrifice in this matter of separate electorates. And I may have to say something more fully on this question at the sessions of the All-India Moslem League where I have been called to preside next Christmas. But the committees appointed by the Congress and the League in

Bombay will soon meet at Calcutta to formulate a scheme of reforms and I most fervently pray that they will both adopt a scheme that may go out to the world as the united demand of India.

One thing is, however, clear. It is not a question of a few more seats going to the Mahomedans or the Hindus. It is a question, as I have already pointed out, in the first instance, of transfer of the power from the bureaucracy to democracy. Let us concentrate all our attention and energy on this question alone for the present.

The Hindus and the Mahomedans should stand united and use every constitutional and legitimate means to effect that transfer as soon as possible. But for a real New India to arise, all petty and small things must be given up.

"She is now India irrendenta and to be redeemed, all Indians must offer up sacrifice not their good things, but all those evil things they cling to blindly—their hates and their divisions, their pride in what they should be thoroughly ashamed of, their quarrels and mis-understandings. These were a sacrifice that God would love."

Now, Ladies and Gentlemen, I have done. In conclusion, let me tell you that, after all, a great deal depends upon ourselves. Hindus and Mahomedans, united and firm, the voice of the three hundred millions of people vibrating throughout the length and the breadth of the country, will produce a force which no power on earth can resist. India has, I believe, turned a corner. She has passed through great sufferings and borne them patiently for centuries. There is now a bright and a great future in front of her. We are on a straight road; the promised land is within sight. "Forward" is the motto and clear course for Young India. But in the onward march, we must be circumspect, and never lose sight of the true perspective before us. And Wisdom and Caution should be our watch-words.

COUNCIL OF INDIA REFORMS.

SPEECH AT THE KARACHI CONGRESS, 1913.

In moving the resolution at the Indian National Congress held at Karachi in December, 1913, under the Presidency of the Hon. Nawab Syed Mahomed, the Hon. Mr. Jinnah said:—

That this Congress is of opinion that the Council of the Secretary of State for India, as at present constituted, should be abolished, and makes the following suggestions for its construction :—

(*a*) That the salary for the Secretary of State for India should be placed on the English estimates.

(*b*) That with a view to the efficiency and independence of the Council it is expedient that it should be partly nominated and partly elected.

(*c*) That the total number of members of the Council should not be less than nine.

(*d*) That the elected portion of the Council should consist of not less than one-third of the total number of members, who should be non-official Indians chosen by a constituency consisting of the elected members of the Imperial and Provincial Legislative Councils.

(*e*) That not less than one-half of the nominated portion of the Council should consist of public men of merit and ability unconnected with Indian administration.

(*f*) That the remaining portion of the nominated Council should consist of officials who have served in India for not less than ten years and have not been away from India for more than two years.

(*g*) That the character of the Council should be advisory and not administrative.

(*h*) That the term of office of each member should be five years.

MR. PRESIDENT, LADIES AND GENTLEMEN,—You do not know what pleasure it gives me to stand on this platform in this city of Karachi where I was born, (cheers), where I have found by me after my arrival at this city personal friends with whom I played in my boyhood, I was delighted to see so many of my Sindhi friends who are here.

Gentlemen, the resolution which I am going to place before you is a resolution on a dull subject. Therefore if you expect any rhetoric or any kind of literary speech from me you will be disappointed. The resolution is this. (See above). Now, Gentlemen, you all know, at least most of you know, that the present Council of the Secretary of State for India, as at present constituted, consists of members who have all served in India in one service or another. That is to say, the India Council which is supposed to be advisory to the Secretary of State consists of officials. That Council is divided into separate groups which are called committees. Each committee has a designation given to it according to the functions of the Secretary of State it performs. You have the political committee, you have the Revenue committee, and these committees are formed principally to advise the Secretary of State on these questions. Now one objection, and that is the strongest against the constitution of the Council, is that it is entirely composed of officials who go from this country. I do not say that officials are, as a class, an undesirable class. But they go from this country, with certain formed opinions of the administration of this country. These are the men who, with their set opinion, formed after years and years service in this country go back to the India Council to advise the Secretary of State who is the head of the Government of India. This is one objection, the second objection is that in this Council there is no place given to the views of the people of India from the non-official point of view. The third objection is that the members of Council guide the Secretary of State for India. The function of the Council should be that of an Advisory Committee.

The Secretary of State for India is for practical purposes the head of the Government of India. He should not be absolutely in the position of figure-head. I think most people will agree with me when I say that the present constitution of the Council makes the Secretary of State a greater Moghul than any Moghul that ruled in India. For this reason the Council should be formed as to able to advise the Secretary of State, and the Council, as at present constituted, should be abolished.

We further submit that the salary of the Secretary of State should be placed on the English estimate. At the present moment the Secretary of State is not responsible to anyone. He can come to any conclusion he likes and is responsible to nobody. Such a state of things is undesirable. We all know that although somewhat late, it is proposed that this Council should now be reformed. The Council was reformed as far back as 1858. It is a wonder to me that it has so long been unreformed. The necessity for reform is obvious. We have got reformed Councils in the different parts of the country. We have in the Imperial Council, Local Councils and even in the Executive Councils non-official members. But the Advisory Council of the

Secretary of State is purely an official body. It is purely an official tribunal.

The Secretary of State has announced that he now proposes to reform the Council. It is better late than never. For that purpose opinion is invited from all parts of the country. It is in the fitness of things that we should express our opinion. The first thing that we say is that this Council should not be changed so far as its character is concerned, namely, this Council should not be administrative, but should remain an Advisory Council. Then our proposal is that it should consist of 9 members and three of them should be Indians chosen by the elected members of the Imperial and Local Councils.

These three members would be in a position to place before the Secretary of State the Indian point of view. We have no desire to deprive the Secretary of State of the services of those men who served in this country in the civil service or any other service. We say that three men from the services in this country should also be elected to the Council. The remaining three should be selected from men of ability, but not connected with the administration of this country. They would be able to advise the Secretary of State regarding matters of this country. It is a reasonable proposition and I hope the Secretary of State will feel that it requires his full consideration.

Gentlemen, I need not detain you any longer. I commend this resolution to your acceptance. (Cheers).

CONGRESS DEPUTATION—LONDON, 1914

Sir William Wedderburn entertained the Congress delegates in London at the Westminster Palace Hotel (May, 1914) and a very large number of gentlemen were present to welcome the delegates, when Mr. Mahomed Ali Jinnah spoke:—

Mr. Mahomed Ali Jinnah said that Lord Crewe had in contemplation a Bill which was intended to reform the India Council—which was really the head of the Government of India and the highest tribunal in all matters executive. It had created a most satisfactory impression in India that an opportunity for stating their views should be given to them by the Government before the Bill was introduced into the British Parliament. At the present moment the India Council was composed of ten members. Two were financial experts, and the rest, who were nominated by the Secretary of State, were connected with the administration of India. Although Lord Morley very recently recognised that anybody who could give first-hand information on Indian matters to his Council would prove very desirable members of that body, and although he gave effect to that view by appointing two Indian members, those two gentlemen were nominated members only, and while they had done excellent work, and had tried, to the best of their ability and judgment, to place the views of the Indian people before the Council, yet something more was desired. It was necessary that the Secretary of State should be kept in intimate touch with the trend of public opinion in India. Men who were connected with the administration and were brought up in the service, were debarred by the virtue of the rules of that very service from attending political meetings, and thereby obtaining the clear insight which was necessary for them to adequately represent Indian opinion. Representatives were required who had been, so to speak, behind the scenes, and men who had been brought up solely in the administrative groove. They wanted on the Council men in touch with public feeling and acquainted with public sentiment and public opinion, and therefore in a position to put before the Secretary of State views which men connected with the service could not possibly do. How were they to secure representatives of the character? Their suggestion was that the only possible way was to introduce the principle of election. Once they got elected members on the Council, they would have representatives who would be responsible for the people of India, and who would not secure re-election if their work had not proved satisfactory. The proposal he had first to submit was that the Council should consist of a minimum number of nine members—one-third of whom should be elected Indians. The principle of election had already been recognised over and over again in regard to this Council. More than one attempt had been made to reform it, and on every occasion the principle of election had been recognised; but the difficulty was to form the electorate. He quite agreed that that presented great difficulty in times gone by, but to-day they had already got an electorate in India which had been working for a number of years. He could best illustrate it by describing what occurred in the Presidencies of Bombay, Madras or Bengal which sent their representatives to the Imperial Council. In the last two elections they had taken place under the new Council Act, and even before, they had chosen their representatives in Bombay to the Imperial Council in this way. The non-official members of the Local Council elected those whom they sent to the Imperial Council.

Thus they had a ready-made electorate in the elected members of the Provincial Councils. Those elected members could choose the members to represent them on the Imperial Council. He thought that would prove a most satisfactory electorate. It would secure the choice of really representative men. The system had already obtained a certificate from eminent officials in India, like Sir Guy Fleetwood Wilson, and the late and the present Viceroy. As to the character of the Council, his suggestion was that it should be advisory and not administrative. It had been given out that the portfolio system was to be introduced. He thought that would be fatal and dangerous. It would mean duplicating the machinery and reducing the Secretary of State to a mere figure-head. If each man was to be placed in charge of a portfolio, and if he was to be necessarily connected with the administration, it would mean that a man who had retired from the service in India, would be called upon to dispose of matters which were the subject of complaint against the very class from which he was drawn. Hitherto, the Secretary of State had not only dealt with matters of detail, but also with matters of principle and policy. It was in the fitness of things that there should be antagonism between the official and the non-official views on these questions—questions, for instance, such as the separation of the Executive from the Judiciary—or the extension of Elementary Education or the Press Act. The Secretary of State, consequently, when these matters came before him would be unable to hear both sides of the question if he had nothing but the official element surrounding him. They wanted the Secretary of State to be made the real master of the situation. They wanted him to be placed in possession of the real facts on both sides. Of course, ultimately, the decision rested with him. The full Council, as they knew, might come to a unanimous conclusion on a particular subject which the Secretary of State might not accept, for he had very wide powers. He further submitted that no distinction should be made between the Indian members of the Council and their colleagues. If any was made they would be demoralizing not only the whole Council but the Indian members as well. It had also been suggested that if they had the portfolio system, they would not be able to get Indian members of the Council with the requisite experience of administration in India, and, therefore, the Indian members would not be able properly to discharge their duties, if placed in charge of a portfolio. It was next suggested that the period of appointment should be five years. While it was necessary to have men with experience in administration, it was equally necessary to have men who could place the public point of view before the Secretary of State. It was proposed that one-third of the Council should consist of the official class, one-third of the non-official class, and the remaining one-third should be men of merit and ability in public life in United Kingdom unconnected with the Indian administration. This third would hold the balance between the two other sections. They would bring to bear upon the deliberations of the Council that independent judgment which was so characteristic of public men in this country. If these proposals were accepted, they would have a Council composed of three different groups—each specialising in a different branch, but all helping the deliberations of the Council over which the Secretary of State presided. The Secretary of State for India, to whatever political party he belonged, had always been an eminent British statesman who had done his best for India; but even the best of men required some kind of control and check. The Secretary of State, no doubt, was responsible to Parliament and the British public in theory, but in practice really he was not responsible; and what was finally suggested was that his salary should be placed upon the British estimates. In that case they would have real effective control by Parliament.

INDIANS IN SOUTH AFRICA.

Passing to discuss the position of the Indians in the various parts of the British Empire, Mr. Jinnah said that no other subject had so deeply stirred the minds of the people of India. They had always understood that they were members of the British Empire, but at this moment they were being denied the rights and privileges of British citizenship. Recent events in South Africa had created intense feeling which was only alleged by the wise and statesmanlike pronouncement of Lord Hardinge; and the action of the Viceroy, supported as it had been, by British ministers and by the British Parliament, had made a deep impression in the hearts of the people of India.

STATEMENT IN "LONDON TIMES", 1914

India is perhaps the only member of the British Empire without any real representation, and the only civilized country in the world that has no real system of representative government.

The news of the intention of reform and reorganising the Council of the Secretary of State for India raised great hopes amongst the people of India, and a very moderate and reasonable demand was put forward that one-third of the total number of the Council should be Indian members, to be elected or chosen by ballot by the elected members of the various Legislative Councils in India. This demand was embodied in the resolutions that were passed by two of the most representative and the greatest organisations of public opinion in India—*viz.*, the Indian National Congress and the All-India Moslem League—at their sessions last Christmas. Further the Indian National Congress, in response to the express desire of Lord Crewe, who was good enough to say that he would welcome any criticism or fresh ideas which might be brought forward on the subject, sent a deputation which waited on him last month, when I had the honor to place my views before him.

Now that the Bill to amend the laws as to the Council of India has been introduced and gone through its first reading, I cannot but say that the provisions contained therein are most disappointing, and I feel sure that that is how the people of India will receive it. What hope can measures like this inspire in the people of India who are looking forward to bigger and more substantial reform in time to come when in matters such as the reform of the Council of the Secretary of State for India, which is, after all, more advisory in its character than anything else, the just proposals of the deputation appointed by the Indian National Congress have not been accepted.

SELECTION OR ELECTION

First of all, there will be only two Indian members, and not one-third of the total number; the minimum number being seven and the maximum ten; so the demand for three Indian members is rejected.

Secondly, the Bill denies the election of the Indian members for all practicable purposes. The Secretary of State for India, under the provisions of the Bill, shall select Indian members from amongst the persons whose names appear on the list of persons domiciled in India, chosen for the purpose by members (other than the official members) of the Legislative Councils, the Governor-General, Governors, Lieutenant Governors and the Chief Commissioner, in such manner, subject to such conditions and restrictions and in such number as may be prescribed by regulations to be made by the Secretary of State for India in Council or by directions issued by the Secretary of State thereunder.

Now, there is no doubt that what appears at the first blush on paper to be some sort of principle of election is for all practical purposes illusory; and the so-called list, or, to put it in other words, panel, is to be formed by the choice of non-official members of various Councils. This sounds as if the officials will have no voice in the choosing of the list or the forming of the panel, but anyone who knows the actual constitution of the various Legislative Councils will see at once that the non-official members means elected as well as members nominated by the Government in various parts of India (that is the officials in the country), and there is a large number of such members in various Councils who are bound in the very nature of things to follow the behest of the official class and this class of nominated members will have a very potent voice in the formation of the panel, to say nothing of a certain element of even elected members who will not be able to exercise free and independent judgment for personal reasons. The consequence of this will be that a large number will get on to that list or panel who would be pure creatures of the official classes and not the representatives of the people, and this might be worse, if the rules, regulations, conditions and restrictions mentioned in the Bill are not most carefully framed. Therefore, what appears on paper to be a list of men chosen by the people will be so in name only; nay, worse, because at present the Indian members are nominated, whereas under the Bill it will be said that they are the representatives of the people, although the selection of the Secretary of State for India might fall on those of the list who may be pure creatures of the official class.

A READY-MADE ELECTORATE.

If the principle of election is to be accepted, why whittle it away by adopting the most circuitous and clumsy methods? By far the simplest way is to form an electorate which is ready-made consisting of all the elected members of the various Councils referred to in the Bill, and let them elect the Indian representatives by ballot. If there is any fear of any undesirable man being elected, for which I do not think there is the slightest ground, I should be willing, if necessary, to give the Secretary of State for India, who is always an eminent statesman whichever party he belongs to, the power to veto it and direct a fresh election in that particular case; but anything short of this will, I feel sure, not satisfy the people of India. With regard to the other provisions of the Bill, it is not very clear as to exactly what is intended, because in introducing the Bill Lord Crewe did not make any statement; but as far as my reading of the clauses goes, I think there is no desire to create a portfolio system. If this be so, then the alarm that was caused in India last year owing to the pronouncement of Lord Crewe, which lent colour to that impression, will, no doubt, be dispelled.

However, I think that the other clauses require some further explanation before one can deal with the provisions contained therein, and, therefore, I do not propose to say anything about them now, but it is most important to see that proper rules and regulations are framed as contemplated by the Bill—(*Times*).

GOKHALE MEMORIAL.

The following is the text of the speech delivered by the Hon. Mr. M. A. Jinnah at a meeting held in Bombay in May, 1915, to commemorate the life and great work of Mr. Gokhale when moving the resolution reading as :—

"That this meeting resolves that a suitable memorial or memorials be raised to commemorate the life and great work of Mr. Gokhale and that a Committee with power to add to their number be appointed to collect subscriptions and to take all necessary measures in that behalf."

This resolution which I have just read to you as for its object the practical way in which we can raise a memorial befitting the great life and work of Mr. Gokhale. I feel confident that Bombay will rise to the occasion and will show her signal mark of appreciation of the work of such a patriot in a manner which will do credit to him as well as to the city of Bombay that claims to be "Urbs Prima in Indis." We mourn the death of Mr. Gokhale so deeply with the rest of India that I have no words at my command to adequately express our deep sorrow and grief. He was respected by the Mahomedans and the Hindus alike and trusted by both. He had endeared himself to all India by his single-mindedness of purpose, his earnestness and zeal with which he worked and his absolute devotion to the cause of India as a whole. He was of late looked upon as an all-India man, if such an expression is permissible. He was a great political rishi, a master of the finance of India and the greatest champion of education and sanitation He was a fearless critic and opponent of the measures of Government and the administration of the country, but in all his action and utterances he was guided by reason and true moderation. Thus he was a help to Government and source of great strength and support to the cause of the people. One of the greatest lessons that his life and work teach one is the example of what one single individual can achieve, how powerfully and materially he can help and guide the destinies of his country and his people, and from whom how millions can derive true lead and inspiration to illustrate this. I have but only to refer to the South African question which stirred the whole of India under his lead. Personally I have had the honour of being one of the colleagues of Mr. Gokhale in the Imperial Council for some years, and to me it was always a matter of pride and pleasure to listen to him and often follow his lead. The whole Council, officials and non-officials, had the greatest respect and regard for him. His loss is difficult to make up. It is almost irreparable. To mark our appreciation of him all we can do now, that the hand of Providence has taken him away from us, is to pray that his mighty soul may rest in peace, and raise a memorial to his life and great work worthy of that great statesman and true patriot, who has passed away. Mr. Gokhale has left millions behind him to mourn his death, but to millions his life and work will be a source of education, example and inspiration, specially to

Young India. Once addressing the students in England he advised them to keep their faces towards India always no matter where they work like the Japanese who always has his face towards "Nipon." Now let me not forget that while we have gathered here to-day to mourn his death, and while the whole of India is doing the same for the past few days what must be the feeling of sorrow and grief of those who are related to him to whom he was nearest and dearest, specially the daughters whom he leaves behind to mourn the death of such a noble power. To them I can say with absolute assurance our deepest and fullest sympathies go out in their great moment of grief. May they have the fortitude to bear such a loss.

INDIAN STUDENTS IN ENGLAND.

A public meeting was held on the 28th June, 1913, at the Caxton Hall, Westminster, to discuss a scheme for the establishment of a Central Association and that in London for Indian students. Mr. H. N. Lall presided.

The Hon. M. A. Jinnah, in moving the resolution as under, spoke as follows .—

This meeting of the Indian students in the United Kingdom resolves that a central society called the London Indian Association be formed with the following aims and objects: (1) To maintain and foster unity, and to strengthen and encourage friendship between the Indian students in the United Kingdom by providing various opportunities for social intercourse, and interchange of thought and ideas by holding (*a*) debates and discussions on various subjects of interest, (*b*) social gatherings, and (*c*) by acquiring a club-house. (2) Provided that this association does not take any part in actual and administrative politics.

Mr. Jinnah said he had spent five or six years as a student in this country, and was now an annual visitor. He had done his best to make himself acquainted with the feelings of Indian students, and had been struck by one remarkable circumstance, they were suffering it seemed to him, from what he might call the bane of India. The caste system—a system which, admirable though it might have been when initiated, was now responsible for the backwardness of their country. In England, they had set up a dozen such societies, but they lack one thing—a central organisation where they could meet together and form friendship. He had found general sympathy with the idea. The position of the Indian students in this country was one without a parallel. They came to England when between the ages of 18 and 23; they were totally separated from their relatives and friends; they were away from the influence of their elders; they had no one to guide them. The Indian student class was typically representative of the best the country could produce, and their action and conduct were inflicted upon their country at home. They were, so to speak, the custodians of the reputation of India. Unfortunately just now, so far as the British public was concerned, they had not a good name. Instead of conducting themselves merely as students and learning all they could of the civilization which the British people had taken centuries to build up they had been tempted to use strong language and take strong action in political question. It may be asked why should their liberty be restricted because of the acts of one or two mad men among them? He agreed that their liberty ought not to be restricted; but he would remind them that they were scarcely competent as yet with the political problem presented by their country. Nobody appreciated more than he did; the honesty of their purpose or the patriotism which had induced them to do what they had done; but it was time for them seriously to consider their position. To take part in politics would simply be to injure their position as students. It was in the light of these views that there was no proposal to include among the objects of the central association participation in politics. Neither did they propose that it should be the duty of the organisation to watch over and safeguard the particular interests of Indian students in Great Britain. They abstained from that deliberately, because they did not want to come into conflict with the authorities in any way. They could not for instance, undertake to fight the case of a student refused admission to an Inn of Court or a University College. They know that the Executive had agents in India who secured the fullest possible information as to students, and although the information might be wrong it was utterly impossible for any association to take up the case of a student unless it could have equally effective means of obtaining knowledge of the student's history. They might ask him: What then was the proposed association to do? They were, in the first place, going to get rid of the exclusiveness which was the outcome of having many different clubs and societies, and they were going to develop the opportunities for a wider national outlook. By communion one with another, by the exchange of ideas, they would come better to understand one another; they would get broader views, they would widen their outlook, and fit themselves for the more responsible duties which would fall on them when they returned home. Today in India the men who were taking the most active part in politics were men who were educated in England and had returned home to serve their country. The students of yesterday were the active politicians of to-day. By all means let them mix with the English people and make friends among them. But let them make it their first duty while they were in this country to meet and understand their own countrymen. It was their presence in England that gave them opportunity of coming into contact with others from all parts of India. If they loved their country, as he was sure they did, they would make this sacrifice. At the same time, the proposed association would give them an opportunity of debating subjects in which all were interested. He did not ask them to eschew political discussion. They would be at liberty to discuss ideas of them, but they must not think of sending the resolutions they agreed upon to the Press or to high Government officials as the views of their association. Finally, they hoped in due time to be able to establish a club house—a permanent house for students of the future as of to-day, and he believed that if they showed their worth, if they went on the lines he was suggesting, there would be no difficulty as to finding the necessary money. They must not give the Government cause to take precautionary measures, and they must observe a high code of honor and morality in this country; they should abandon strong language and hysterical ideas, become earnest workers and serious thinkers, and then they could hope to go back home as great missionaries in the cause of progress.

BOMBAY MOSLEM STUDENTS' UNION

At a meeting of the Bombay Muslim Students' Union on the 13th February, 1915, Mr. M. A Jinnah, delivering the inaugural address, said:—

The mere fact that this Union was formed was a distinct sign of progress so far as the Mahomedans were concerned. Their constitution was admirable and he congratulated them on the support they had been able to secure and the results they had so far achieved. But he asked them to remember that though it might be an easy thing to form an association, it was not always easy to work one. He always took the greatest interest in students, and, therefore, when the Secretary asked him to say a few words at this meeting he gladly accepted the invitation. Continuing, Mr. Jinnah said, one of the foremost things they had to bear in mind was the value of discipline. If they wanted to make this Union useful, they must go through regular discipline in all they did in connection with it, so that it might be useful to them in the wider life which awaited them when their student days were over.

WANTED UNITY AND GOOD-WILL

The second point he wished to emphasise was that if their association was going to be built on a permanent foundation, they must learn to practice self-reliance. Then again one of their chief objects should always be co-operation, unity and good-will, not only among the different sections of Mahomedans but also between the Mahomedan and other communities of this country. (Loud Applause). As citizens they would have to share the burden of work, when their student days were over, with other communities, and it would be therefore better if they started at the earliest possible opportunity to try to understand the other communities. That would be the surest way of progress in the country, and there were sure signs of this progress. But there was one thing which must be realised by every thinking person as essential. If progress was to be made, it would not be by dissensions. Unity was absolutely essential to progress.

He earnestly appealed to them to do away with dissensions with all their might.

"BE A TRUE PATRIOT."

Then again it was necessary to settle the course of their own progress. The present system of education was not exactly one that led to that road But notwithstanding all difficulties, he asked them to bear in mind one thing, namely, that everyone of them should be a true patriot. (Loud applause). They must understand the current affairs of the country. They often heard people saying that they took no interest in politics. For himself, he could not understand an educated man saying he could take no interest in politics. Politics had in some quarters assumed a definition that was anything but true. It did not necessarily mean agitation. A man could take interest in politics without participating in agitation. And even if a man did take part in agitation it did not mean that he wanted to pull down the government. He did not advocate students taking an active part in politics, but he urged that they must, as early as possible, take an interest in and understand politics.

In India politics had become the life-blood of the people (applause) and it was therefore no use their shutting their eyes to it. In conclusion he said they must work the Students' Union in such a manner that this membership would convey the idea of refined gentlemen of great principles and convictions, of upright men passionately fond of their country, of men who, when they finished their student days, would enter upon their wider life with the determination of carrying out those principles and convictions and standing by and following them even at great sacrifice. (Loud applause).

VOTE OF CONFIDENCE IN LORD HARDINGE.

A public meeting was held under the joint auspices of the Bombay Branches of the Home Rule League, (July, 1917), at the Morarji Goculdas Hall, Cavel Street, Bombay, to pass a resolution of confidence in Lord Hardinge. The Hon. Mr. M. A. Jinnah presided and there was a large attendance.

The President said —This meeting was called, as they knew, for the purpose of recording their confidence in Lord Hardinge. Before he addressed them on this subject he must express to the members of the League his sincere thanks for the honour they had done him by electing him their President. Turning to the subject he said they must have read in the papers the statement which Lord Hardinge had made in the House of Lords and he (the speaker) was sure they all would agree with him that he conveyed the universal feeling on the part of educated India that Lord Hardinge's appeal had entered deeply into their hearts. (Applause). Lord Hardinge had appealed, for a verdict on his administration, not only to British public opinion but also to Indian public opinion. (Applause). He (Lord Hardinge) had said that India had been *bled white* to help the allies and that it was India whose help at a most critical moment of the war, saved Europe. (Applause). He (the speaker) was sure he was voicing the feeling not only of this meeting but also of the general public that it was due to the fact of there being a statesman of Lord Hardinge's character and a Viceroy of his calibre, who held the confidence of the people of this country and who understood the pulse of the public of India, that it had been possible to send the troops to France at a most critical stage of the war, and it was Lord Hardinge alone that could have achieved what he did then by sending the troops. In his own words India was "bled white" and submitted to all sacrifices without a murmur at that critical time. Why was it, the speaker asked, that even now India was willing to bleed white without a murmur? It was because they had

had a Viceroy who shared in their sorrows and who shared in their joys, (applause), who understood the hearts of the people of this country, and who held liberal and generous ideas about their national progress. It was therefore that they met there that afternoon to show their confidence in Lord Hardinge.

THEN AND NOW.

He (the speaker) could not help striking this note that while they had a Viceroy like Lord Hardinge at that juncture and that while to-day also India was in the same frame of mind as she was then and was ready to make any sacrifices that she might be called upon to make for the British Empire, (applause), still it was an unfortunate thing that a policy of repression was now being pursued in various provinces. It was unfortunate that not only a policy of repression was pronounced and carried out by the different provincial pro-consuls but also it was still more regrettable that the present Viceroy was maintaining a studied silence in the cloudy regions of Simla when India was stirred to its very depths. He hoped these humble words of his would penetrate the cloudy regions of Simla and reach the ears of the Viceroy, who should understand that India was really true and loyal to the Empire. (Applause).

PROTEST AGAINST INTERNMENTS

At a crowded mass meeting convened under the auspices of the Bombay Presidency Association on 30th July, 1917, the Hon. Mr M. A. Jinnah, who presided, addressing the assembly, said.—

This Public Meeting of the citizens of Bombay is called to express its emphatic protest against the actions and policy of some of the Provincial Governments in India and against the Government of India for allowing such actions to be taken and such a policy to be pursued and remaining studiously silent, while the country at large is stirred to its very depth. Ladies and Gentlemen, it seems obvious that, if we accept the policy of the Government, all constitutional and lawful agitation will, in effect, be stopped, that the freedom of speech and the press and the right of public meeting under the British flag is henceforth to be regulated by the arbitrary judgment and decision of a Provincial Governor or Government, that the Executive are to decide what is lawful and constitutional propaganda without reference to the Courts of Justice of His Majesty the King-Emperor. Is this the aim and object of those who are responsible for the actions of the Provincial Government?

It is said that we are to put out of our thoughts entirely the early grant of Self-Government to India, that we are not going to get anything like the reforms formulated and sanctioned by the Indian National Congress and the All-India Moslem League last December at Lucknow to be given effect to at the close of the War, that we must be content with small minor reforms which the Bureaucracy have recommended though we are not yet even accorded the small mercy of knowing what they are—that we are not to raise expectations in the minds of the people which are not going to be fulfilled. We are threatened with Government action if we do not obey these warnings—and as an earnest thereof Mrs. Besant and her co-workers are interned—any expression of public opinion recording disapproval of the Government action is not desired. In Bengal and Delhi public meetings have been stopped already. Now why is India alone of all other parts of the Empire to be marked out for silence—and why should we be at this moment subjected to this repressive policy? We are shedding our blood and pouring our money ungrudgingly and unstintingly for the defence of the Empire in this War, the very basis of which is to preserve the liberty and freedom of people of various countries. Is the Bureaucracy of India blind? Have they lost their reason to treat loyal India at this juncture in this manner? It is a mistake. It shows an utter want of wisdom and statesmanship. What is His Excellency the Viceroy Lord Chelmsford doing? His silence at this moment is most ominous and worse than the most drastic repressive actions already adopted and enforced by some of the Provincial Governments.

PROTEST AGAINST INTERNMENTS

We protest against the internments of Mrs. Besant and her co-workers not only on principle, but also because it is an attempt to intern the Home Rule or Self-Government Scheme of reforms framed and adopted conjointly by the Indian National Congress and the All-India Moslem League at Lucknow. We declare that we stand by that Scheme unswervingly and unflinchingly, and we shall do all that lies in our power for its realisation at the close of the War. We protest against the methods adopted and attempts that are made, to silence the people of India from carrying on their constitutional agitation. We feel that Government are blind to the real public opinion in the country regarding the Reform Scheme passed at Lucknow; and are entirely misled and pursuing a policy which is fraught with most serious consequences. It has already led the people to earnestly consider whether they should not adopt the principle and methods of Passive Resistance.

AN UNPRECEDENTED AND A MOST UNFORTUNATE SITUATION.

The present political situation is unprecedented and most unfortunate; it has cast the gravest responsibility upon the leaders, the people and the Government alike, which requires the most careful and immediate attention of us all. Let us not try to muddle through as usual. The times are different and changed. We require at once a clear and definite enunciation of the policy of the Government. We require that the confidence of the people in the Government which has been so severely shaken within the past three months should be restored at once to enable us to win this war, which has been our first and foremost consideration throughout this long and weary struggle which has been going on for nearly three years The people of India are anxious to help onward the progress of their country and are earnestly endeavouring to attain the status of a Self-Governing Member of the Empire at an early date, but it is really a folly to think that because of that they are not loyal to the Empire. For the matter of that I say that educated Indians are as loyal to the Crown and the Empire as any Englishman is. I trust that statesmen of the calibre of the Prime Minister, Mr Lloyd George, and the Secretary of State for India, Mr. Montagu, who are at the head of the Government of

England and India, will not allow this situation to assume a still more serious character.

In the belief and faith that British statesmanship has not come to the point of utter bankruptcy, I appeal to it on behalf of this meeting that they should not lose any time in making a declaration of policy for making India a Self-Governing Member of the British Empire at an early date, and order the reversal of the recent repressive policy, in response to the public opinion which is unequivocal and emphatic throughout the country.

HOME RULE.

At a meeting held under the auspices of the Allahabad Home Rule League on October, 1917, the Hon'ble Mr. Jinnah said:—

I wish to say why it was that I joined the Home Rule League. When representations were made and resolutions passed year after year by the National Congress when their demands were pressed last year in that carefully drafted memorandum of the 19 members of the Imperial Council, it was said that that was only the demand of a few educated agitators and lawyers, but that the masses were not ready for any such reform. It was to meet that attack which was made in this country as well as in England, it was to remove that misrepresentation that they resolved that there should be an educative propaganda and that they should reach the masses and put the verdict of the masses not only before the bureaucracy but before the democracy of Great Britain and I am happy to find not less than 10,000 persons (Cries of 'more than 10,000') have come here for the purpose of vindicating their claim, to show that not only a few educated agitators and lawyers but the masses wanted this reform. By pressing their demand they had brought about a distinct and definite change in the policy of Government. I do not wish to use an expression which had been used that the Government had climbed down, but I will say that the Government were convinced that the people of India were not going to tolerate the present state of administration, and they demanded a substantial share in the administration of the country, and his Majesty's Government had definitely decided to send Mr. Montagu to this country. He was coming here to see what was the force behind the demands that they made in the 19 members' memorandum and the Congress-League scheme. We have to face Mr. Montagu and three powerful opponents in this country, and I want you to be prepared for that. Those three opponents are firstly our bureaucracy. As Mr. Tilak pointed out, the bureaucracy had enjoyed a monopoly of power in the administration of the country. It was natural that they were unwilling to part with it. The second class of opponents are the members of the Anglo-Indian commercial community who had enjoyed the monopoly of commerce and exploited this country for now over two centuries. What did this community mean when they said, that they had a stake in this country? What was their stake? They said that they had invested a large amount of capital in this country. Only the other day I was trying to find out the total British capital invested all over the world and I found that the total British capital so invested was roughly 1,700 millions. Out of this only 300 millions were invested in British India, and a large part was invested in countries where the English people had no voice in the government: such as Russia, Japan, Persia, Argentine, etc. And yet we were told that so long as the 300 millions remained invested here they, the sons of the soil, who had got their homes, their property, everything here, should remain under the control of the bureaucracy for ever. I say this is a fictitious argument. This is an argument which is intended to avoid the issue. I do not admit that that capital would be in danger. Nobody asked for any revolutionary changes in the administration of the country. It is an absolute humbug and sham to say that if the reforms we demand were granted then British capital here would not be secure. Then there was a third element, unfortunately again a monopoly, that was the military. I am very glad—I acknowledge freely—that His Majesty's Government had decided to throw open the commissioned ranks to the sons of the country, but there again, as Mr. Tilak put it, that admission must be a real one and not a shadowy one. They are our opponents and I would ask every one of you to be ready and do all that lies in your power and be prepared to convince Mr. Montagu and demolish these monopolies.

THE PRESENT EUROPEAN AGITATION

Under the joint auspices of the Branches of the Home Rule League a public meeting was held in Shantaram's Chawl, in November 1917 the Hon. Mr. M A. Jinnah presiding. The subject was "The Present European Agitation," and there was a very large gathering:—

The Chairman said they were met to hear three prominent citizens who would address them on the question of the European agitation in this country. Referring to various statements which had appeared in the "Statesman" and other papers, Mr. Jinnah said · I really do not understand what they mean. It only shows that they are absolutely ignorant of the demands that we are making. If they only understood what was the scheme of reforms adopted by the Congress and the All-India Moslem League I am quite sure they would never advance such futile arguments. What I for myself would like to know from the Anglo-Indian community in this country is this. They admit that reforms must be introduced but they must be constitutional, they must be reasonable and they must be gradual. What I want to know is: What are the reforms which they propose to introduce into this country? We have not heard anything yet about it. There is one more word which I would like to say before I introduce the first speaker. Lord Sydenham, that reactionary who enjoyed the hospitality of this country and earned a fat salary from the coffers of its exchequer, has been carrying on an agitation (Cries of Shame) which is discreditable to any man. He says as soon as the masses, for whom we are the trustees, are fit for Self-Government, we shall instantly hand over the Government to the people. Well, Gentlemen, all I can say is this. When the masses are fit for Self-Government they will not go to Lord Sydenham for Self-Government. That is my answer to Lord Sydenham.

The first speaker in the programme to-day is Mr. Bomanji who, as you know, is one of our strongest pillars. (Cheers). It was Mr. Bomanji who gave us the munificent gift of one lakh of rupees at a critical moment. He is not a lawyer like myself, but is a commercial magnate and the reply to the European commercial community should come from him and you will hear when he addresses what the reply is.

CONCLUDING SPEECH

Gentlemen, a special feature of to-day's meeting which has struck me is that every one of our principal speakers are members of the commercial community and it is but in the fitness of things that to the commercial attack there shall be a commercial counter-attack because remember that the one thing that has come out very clearly in the discussion which was put before you by the various merchants of position, experience and reputation was this, that the Europeans wished to maintain the commercial monopoly in this country and it is up to our merchants like Mr. Bomanji and the others who followed him that that monopoly should not be tolerated in this country and it is up to them to fight that battle which we have been fighting all this time for them. The time has come for them now to come to our rescue and reinforce us with the power which the Indian commercial world possesses at this moment in this country. It is only by their help and support that we shall be able to meet our opponents successfully.

Now I thank you very much for the warm reception you gave to the vote of thanks. My message to-day is this. I find in this meeting to-day a number of Musalmans and I am very happy to see them here. (Cheers.)

My message to the Musalmans is to join hands with your Hindu brethren. My message to the Hindus is to lift your backward brother up. In that spirit let the foundation of the Home Rule League be consecrated and there is nothing to fear for us. (Loud and continued cheers.)

THE CONGRESS-LEAGUE SCHEME.

In moving the following resolution of the Congress-League Scheme at the session of the All-India Moslem League held at Calcutta in December, 1917, viz :

(a) That the All-India Muslim League records its sense of great satisfaction at the announcement made by His Majesty's Secretary of State for India in the House of Commons on the 20th August, 1917, that the policy of His Majesty's Government is "that of increasing the association of Indians in every branch of administration and gradual development of self-governing institutions, with a view to progressive realisation of Responsible Government in India as an integral part of the British Empire."

(b) That in redemption of the pledge made in the announcement, "that substantial steps in this direction should be taken as soon as possible," the League strongly urges upon the Government the immediate introduction of a

Bill embodying the reforms contained in the Congress-League Scheme of December, 1916, as the first step towards the realisation of Responsible Government and fix a time limit in the statute itself within which complete Responsible Government should be established in India, provided always that the principle adequate and effective representation of Moslem community is made a "sina qua non" *in any scheme of reform," the Hon'ble Mr. Jinnah spoke as follows :—*

This is the most important resolution of all except the one which related to the release of Mr. Mahomed Ali and Mr. Shawkut Ali. The resolution says, in the first instance, that we want Responsible Government to be established in this country within a period, the time limit of which was to be fixed in the statute. I will explain to you what this means. We all know that His Majesty's Government made a pronouncement on the 20th of August. It was the first time in the history of India that the British Government has definitely and clearly declared that the goal of British Rule in this country is to establish Responsible Government. (Hear,

hear). But as against that we had got the pronouncement that it would have to be achieved by successive stages, and substantial steps in that direction would be taken as soon as possible. What we wish to express in this resolution is this, that whatever those stages might be, after substantial steps were taken in that direction, the achievement of complete responsible self-government must be within the time limit which must be fixed in the statute itself. We might ask why we state this. I wish to explain to you why we state that. We state that because we do not wish that the matter should be left to the caprice or the will of the Government, but that we want it in their statute. The second part of the resolution is that towards that goal a definite step should be taken and that step is embodied in the resolution that was passed at the joint meeting of the Congress and the Moslem League. That scheme had been criticised. Many faults have been pointed out by our opponents—many defects have been pointed out to us by our opponents. I wish to say this—and I believe I am expressing the views of the people of India —before them. The first question I wish to put before our opponents is this. Is India to be governed for the good of her people or not? I take it that no honest man be he Englishman or any other, would dare say that India is not to be governed for the good of the people in the first and primary instance. If the proposition is sound then the next proposition is this. If India is to be governed for the good of the people, who is to govern India? Certainly no class, no section, no community, but the people of this country (hear, hear). I recognise ungrudgingly that the British nation has contributed towards what modern India is. But I refuse—and I emphatically refuse —to say that therefore the English people should have monopoly of power here (hear, hear).

A BOGEY.

It is said that we are going on at a tremendous speed, that we are at a minority and that it might afterwards become a

Hindu Government. I want to give an answer to that. I particularly wish to address my Mahomedan friends on this point. Do you think, in the first instance, as to whether it is possible that this country could become a Hindu Government? Do you think that Government could be conducted by ballot boxes? Do you think that because the Hindus are in the majority, therefore they would carry on a measure, in the legislative assembly and there is an end of it? If seventy millions of Mussalmans do not approve of a measure, which is carried by a ballot box, do you think that it could be enforced and administered in this country? (Cries of "no, no")? Do you think that the Hindu statesmen, with their intellect, with their past history, would ever think of—when they get self-government—enforcing a measure by ballot box (cries of "no, no")? Then what is there to fear (cries of "nothing"). Therefore I say to my Moslem friends not to fear. This is a bogey, which is put before you by your enemies (cries of "hear, hear") to frighten you to scare you, away from the co-operation with the Hindus which is essential for the establishment of self-government (cries of "hear, hear"). If this country is not to be governed by the Hindus, let me tell you in the same spirit, it was not to be governed by the Mahomedans either and certainly not by the English (cries of "certainly not"). It is to be governed by the people (cries of "hear, hear") and the sons of this country (cries of "hear, hear") and I, standing here, I believe that I am voicing the feeling of the whole of India—say that what we demand is the immediate transfer of the substantial power of Government of this country (cries of "hear, hear") and that is the principal demand of our scheme of reform.

THE POSITION OF OPPONENTS.

Do not our opponents understand this? Are they so dull? Are they so foolish? Do they not understand this demand? Our demand is this "you have monopoly in this country in the government of this country. You have monopoly in this country in the army. You have monopoly in the commerce of this country." We are not going to submit to any of these three monopolies. You have enjoyed them for the last 150 years, but we are tired of it" (cries of "hear, hear"). These are the arguments which are advanced by our opponents. They might look very nice on paper, but, believe me that they perfectly well understand us, and they have understood us, but, as it is said, none are so blind as those who won't see. That is their position. They won't see. But fortunately for us—I am very glad to say that the British statesmen have realised the position and the Cabinet, has made a pronouncement and they have sent Mr. Montagu, Secretary of State for India, to this country with a view that he should see for himself what the position is. Mr. Montagu is amongst us and I believe I am expressing the universal feeling of the people of this country when I say this:—We have great faith in him (cries of "hear, hear,") and we trust and hope that he will not fail. All that we can say now to the Government is this—when I say Government I do not mean bureaucratic Government, but I mean His Majesty's Government in England—that we have, after deliberate, careful consideration with all the intelligence and skill that we could possess, produced a scheme and mind you do not say that this is a perfect scheme, but then I challenge any one who can produce a perfect scheme. We say here are our proposals and up to the present moment in this country there is nobody, no association and no individual that has produced a different scheme except Mr. Curtis. I will say what I have got to say with regard to Mr. Curtis' scheme. So far as His Majesty's Government is concerned, I feel this. These are my proposals. At the present moment I have no reason of any kind whatsoever to deviate from this proposal a hair's breadth, because I believe in them. Will you produce what is your proposal? Will you tell me what you are going to do as a substantial step, or substantial steps towards establishing the complete responsible government in this country and if Mr. Montagu —it is no use of my saying it, but I must say it because I am dealing with the subject—

we are fortunate because Mr. Montagu is one of the ablest statesmen of England to-day, publishes his proposals and when he will publish his proposals, as he must, because that has been promised by that famous announcement, and if those proposals are better or more substantial or more in the interest of my country, I can give an assurance to Mr. Montagu and to His Majesty's Government that we are not so foolish as not to accept something of which we are convinced that it is better. But give me your proposal. Give me time to consider and I shall then decide. As far as I know—and I believe it is correct—that Mr. Montagu will probably make his pronouncement before May or before the end of May, (cries of "hear, hear"). The question that I want you to consider to-day is a very important one.

SPECIAL SESSION OF LEAGUE SUGGESTED.

We are passing this resolution, namely, that these are our claims of reforms which we want. But when these proposals are published we must be ready, we must be prepared, at that moment to consider those proposals and I want to make before you—as I said in the Indian National Congress that the Indian National Congress should hold a special sessions to consider those proposals—the same suggestion, which I hope and trust you will approve of namely that we also ought to call a special sessions of the All-India Moslem League to consider those proposals. After we have considered those proposals and we shall do so most willingly in consultation with the Indian National Congress and if ever that moment arise, as I hope it will, that these two bodies call their special meetings and we came to an agreement that this is what we want, this is what we agree upon, then after that I take it that the Hindus and Mahomedans as one nation will make that demand and there will be no going back from it (hear, hear). If you think that you are going to get political freedom or political liberty without some sacrifice, I think you are mistaken (hear, hear). You must remember that there are so many forces working, so many conflicting elements that exist. You must remember that the success or the failure with regard to your demand will depend entirely upon yourself, and the question is what you are capable of doing.

THE TWO ESSENTIALS.

I say you must make up your mind—you must determine that you will not be satisfied —you will never be satisfied with any proposal that the Government may publish unless and until two definite proposals are embodied in those proposals; the first, which is the most potent, and which is the only test of power, is the power of the purse. We want financial control and we want control over the executive. The next thing that I want to say is this. I think I have told you that our opponents understand us. But if they do not understand us I will put before them once more very shortly what we want. The first thing that I want is that all sinister race distinctions should be abolished. It is a stain on our statute books that there should be race distinctions in the eyes of law and justice. That must be abolished instantaneously. (Hear, hear). The second thing I want our opponents clearly to understand is that all coercive measures, which have found their place in the statute books, should be repealed instantaneously. (Hear, hear). The British Government, or no Government in this world, expect people to be loyal to that Government when that Government treats one subject differently from another subject of its The Europeans in this country is not only treated differently by the executive but by the law of the land (cries of "shame"). Does any Government expect that these men, whose history is as great as that of any other nation, whose literature is as noble as that of any other nations in the world, with proper opportunities, and proper education, do not feel the distinctions which are galling in this country at every step? Do they expect the people to remain loyal to this Government where they feel the distinction in every branch, in every walk of life?

COERCIVE MEASURES

The second point that I mention is about the coercive measures. Only take the history of this country of the last twenty years or so. Let us ask this question—what has been the cause of these coercive measures such as the Press Act. The people of this country have been loyal—the people of this country have always been satisfied notwithstanding the many disabilities, many disadvantages and ill-treatments. What is the cause of this? The cause of it you know it, I know it and the Government knows it—is that the people of India resent the continual slavish conditions which prevail in this country. Instead of Government meeting the complaints of the people what do they do in this country? They want to muzzle you. They say we pass Press Act. If you write anything we will, they say, strangle you. They have passed the Seditious Meeting Act to stop meetings of the people. Is this really the method by which you can continue governing people (cries of "certainly not")? Is it possible for any statute to destroy the soul of the people (cries of "no, no")? Instead of meeting the grievances of the people, instead of trying to remedy the defects, they go on passing statutes. I say this is a short-sighted, mistaken policy—it is a blunder and the sooner you realised it the better for you. The next thing what we want is not a few posts. It is not only judgeship and membership of the executive councils, what we want is not that we should be sent there as elected members to advise Government, but we want to have our finger in the pie and very much so. We say transfer the monopoly of power which you have denied to us hitherto—which you have denied to me and my own country. You have no right to do so. Do not put forward arguments which are untruthful—"that you are trustees of the masses" (Hear, hear). Do not put forward arguments in the interest of the masses that the transfer should not be effected. I say it is untruthful argument. (A cry "quite untrue"). They know it. Whom do you believe are the people who say that? Lord Sydenham. What did Lord Sydenham say? He conceded the other day "we are the trustees of the masses". (A cry "He is not still the Governor of Bombay and still is he the trustee"?) You are only a few discontented educated people and you want to establish oligarchy in this country. You do not care for your people at all. But Lord Sydenham sitting in London does. As soon as his five years were over—after taking a very fat salary, for five years—he has become trustee of the masses, having gone to England and is now looking after the masses from there and has become President of the Association. And what is that Association? Other minor trustees, who came here temporarily exciled from their hearth and home came here, which is a terrible country put up all sorts of inconveniences in the ball rooms (laughter) in the clubs which are palatially furnished, in the tennis Courts (laughter) which must be attended to at 4 o'clock (laughter) are the members of the Association and if you please they are drawing a handsome pension good many of them from here (laughter) I know that there is a certain amount of humbug in the clubs, but there must be a limit to it. I think I have done with this question of transfer and I sincerely trust and hope that the press, who are represented here will convey to our opponents, who have not understood us up to the present moment. If this power is transferred there is one thing which I must tell you. I see so many of merchants here several merchants are here and I want to say a few words to them. I hope they will carry that to their fellow merchants. We have been carrying on this agitation certainly for 32 years. Since the Indian National Congress came into existence—and of course our merchants, wealthy people and landed proprietors—I am very glad to see one of their noble examples here—never took any interest—in it. They never bothered their heads. But I speak to the merchants of India, who are the greatest opponents of our demands to-day—the commercial community. Have you realised that? And why? Because with their hoarded capital—which they say that ·they have invested here not more than 4 millions all told they have exploded the commerce and industry of this country. I see that somebody is not quite convinced there—he is shaking his head. Have you any doubt? Any one of you? (cries of "no, no"). Do you not think that it is high time that you.

do your duty and rally round our force, come round the men who have fought that battle more in the interest of commerce and industry remembering that commerce and industry is the backbone of a nation or a country. I do not care for Government posts. I ask my Mahomedan friends, particularly in Bengal. I notice that in Bengal there is no commerce in your hand. What little you have in Bengal you find with the Mahomedans coming from the other parts—very few in this part. It is much more important to pay attention to that. I say that when I have an opportunity given to me in the Government of my country? I have sufficiently shown that—I have publicly shown and repeatedly shown by resolutions which we have passed year after year in the Indian National Congress what are the measures and what are the grievances that require our attention and we say pay your attention to the masses and our grievances. Now with regard to Mr. Curtis' scheme. Mr. Curtis has put forward a scheme. All that I can point out to you at the present moment, because I do not wish to go into the details of it, probably I shall when I meet Mr. Curtis myself, is that scheme is on the face of it one which no self-respecting nation or people can accept (hear, hear). What does he say? He says this. He is going to establish responsible government by compartments, that is to say one compartment bereaucratic Government — another compartment — responsible government and the compartment which will be responsible government will be the minor department with some trifling things such as roads, bridges, drains. He says you shall have complete responsible government established with regard to this department. Now responsible government if it has any meaning it means this, that the executive is liable to be removed by the vote of the legislative or impliedly by the electorate. We shall elect our minister or ministers who will be in charge of that department. This minister in charge of the minor departments will be elected by whom? By the representative Government? I will take the Imperial Council of India first. When we have elected these ministers of ours and when we have placed them in charge of those departments and when you have gone through that experience, says Mr. Curtis then you will be judged—by whom? By the bureaucracy, in what way, whether your power should not be cancelled (laughter) or whether you may be given a little more. I refuse to be judged by the bureaucracy when I sent the best intellect of my country to the Legislative Council, I refuse to be judged by anybody much less the bureaucracy and I refuse that scheme because to my mind it is childish.

SELF-GOVERNMENT FOR INDIA.

The Hon. Mr. Jinnah in seconding the Self-Government Resolution at the 32nd Indian National Congress held at Calcutta in December 1917, said:

It was composed of three parts. The first part expressed its grateful satisfaction over the pronouncement made by the Secretary of State. In 1915 the Congress at Bombay demanded a declaration to this effect. In 1916 the Congress and the Moslem League at Lucknow prepared a joint scheme of reform and desired a declaration of the policy by the Government to the effect that Responsible Self-Government would be conferred at an early date. In response to it the pronouncement was made in Parliament and for that pronouncement they expressed their grateful satisfaction. The second part of the resolution was important. They desired that provision for the establishment of Responsible Self-Government by an enactment of Parliament. They also desired that a time-limit should also be laid. The third step was the granting of complete Self-Government by statute. The speaker next said that it had been stated that the Congress-League scheme contained some novel feature. It had also been said that it was illogical and was capable of creating a deadlock. His answer was that His Majesty's Government had made a pronouncement that the goal was the conferment of complete Self-Government, and they demanded that steps should be taken immediately towards it. They had produced a scheme and they wanted to know what the scheme of the Government was. Up till the present moment they had received no proposal from the Government. Unless they heard to the contrary he thought theirs was the best scheme.

FALLACY OF CURTIS' SCHEME

Referring to Mr. Curtis' proposal he said the bureaucracy would be the judge of the representatives of the people who would be entrusted with the working of certain departments. The bureaucracy would say that in their opinion the people's representatives had abused their power. They could not accept such a scheme and they stood by the Congress-League scheme, until the Government had prepared a scheme which would be considered reasonable.

In conclusion, Mr. Jinnah said that he understood that Mr. Montagu would probably make his pronouncement in England soon after his return, possibly in May. When these proposals came to India what were they going to do? The speaker wanted them to be prepared for that. Those proposals would probably be published in India in May. His view was that as the occasion was momentous and the issue was grave, as soon as the proposals were published in India, there should be a special session of the Congress and the Moslem League to consider the proposals of Mr. Montagu and to make up their mind in the light of those proposals. After that they would put all the power and energy they possessed to back their conclusions up.

THE MOSLEM LEAGUE.

11th NOVEMBER, 1915

The following is the text of an appeal by Mr. Jinnah to the Moslem leaders to assemble largely at the Bombay session of the All-India Moslem League, 1916.

Now that the Council of the All-India Moslem League has decided to hold the Session of the League in Bombay, may I appeal to the Mahomedan leaders of the community in general to close our ranks? We are bound by our constitution. Reverence for and obedience to that constitution and discipline are absolutely necessary qualities to enable us to say that we are fit for real political franchise, freedom and Self-Government.

At this juncture we are watched not only by India but by the whole of the British Empire of which we aspire to be an independent, free and equal member along with the dominions who already enjoy freedom and Self-Government. No consideration of any kind or nature whatsoever should weigh with us or influence us except the best interest of the country and the community. The Indian National Congress and the All-India Moslem League both have for their goal the attainment of Self-Government for India. The recognition of this claim will have to be judged,—and depend greatly upon how the Congress and the League organise control and conduct themselves this year and in the near future.

I wish to state with the greatest emphasis that there is no truth in the baseless statements made in some quarters that any responsible Mahomedan leader thinks that the League should be merged into the Indian National Congress. But conference, in collaboration, if possible, is the object, and what objection is there to this course?

Now that the majority of the leading representatives of the Council have decided on holding the Sessions in Bombay can we not bury our differences, show a united front and acquit ourselves with credit and honour?

What will the success of the Sessions of the League this year mean?

1. It will show the power of organisations, the solidarity of Mussalman opinions and their true worth This will entitle them to claim the rights and privileges of a free people.

2. It will make our Hindu friends value us all the more and will make them feel more than ever that we are worthy of standing shoulder to shoulder with them for the cause and the Motherland.

3. It will prove to British politicians and statesmen, to Parliament and the British nation generally that we are not crying for the moon when we ask for Self-Government but that we are determined and are in earnest about it and that we shall pursue our course steadfastly and unitedly till the goal is realized.

4. It will convince the Government here and in England and the British Empire at large that Mahomedans of India, notwithstanding their religious sentiments and feelings at this juncture of the greatest crisis that the Empire has to face, can show due control, restraint and moderation in their deliberations and can exercise judgment and

pursue a course which is worthy of the highest statesmanship.

In conclusion, I urge all the Mahomedans to rally round the flag of the All-India Moslem League and as true patriots stand by its constitution and thus make the community feel proud of the only political organisations it possesses at present.

MR JINNAH'S REPLY TO MR CASSAMALLI.

BOMBAY, Nov 19, 1915.

Dear Mr Cassamalli,

I am in receipt of yours of 17th instant, and I thank you very much for it.

With regard to your P. S. I do not think you need have any apprehension that the League will include "any impossible demands for self-government." I may however point out to you the objects of the League with which no doubt, you are already familiar, particularly clause D; we must stand by that.

Section 2 says that the object of the League shall be:—

(*a*) to maintain and promote among the people of this country feelings of loyalty towards the British Crown;

(*b*) to protect and advance the political and other rights and interests of the Indian Musalmans;

(*c*) to promote friendship and union between the Mussalmans and other communities of India;

(*d*) without detriment to the foregoing objects, attainment under the ægis of the British Crown, of a system of self-government suitable to India through constitutional means by bringing about, amongst others, a steady reform of the existing system of administration, by promoting national unity, by fostering public spirit among the people of India, and by co-operating with other communities for the said purposes.

(Sd.) M. A. JINNAH.

THE PRESENT POLITICAL SITUATION SEPTEMBER, 1917.

The Hon. Mr. M. A. Jinnah, interviewed on the present political situation in India, said —

The selection of Mr. Montagu to be the Secretary of State for India has given, as was but natural, the people of this country great satisfaction, and the Prime Minister deserves our best thanks for his choice at the present critical juncture. Mr. Montagu knows India already and we are sure of his sympathies for our ideals and aspirations, although India of to-day is greatly changed. This pronouncement which is understood in India as recognising the aspirations of the Indian people of the early grant of Self-Government within the Empire is most welcome and his decision, whatever may be the causes that led to it, namely, to come to India and examine and ascertain the present political situation, is no doubt received with great approval. But in order to ensure the success of his mission before Mr. Montagu sets to work at his task, there should be, in my opinion, a general amnesty declared and all those interned as political prisoners released, and I hope that Lord Chelmsford at whose invitation the Secretary of State for India is coming to this country will respond to the public feeling and sentiment on this matter, which is very strong indeed. The internment of Mrs. Besant is universally resented not only on principle, but because it is understood in view of the pronouncements of the heads of Provincial administrations to be a direct blow to the general national movement in this country, and this was the cause that led the people to consider the question of Passive Resistance.

NEED FOR IMMEDIATE WORK

Repression with one hand and concessions with the other is a policy which no self-respecting people can accept. We are determined to stand by the principles of the memorandum of the 19 members of the Council, and the Reform Scheme of the Congress and the Moslem League, and I would urge upon the leaders and every organization and the people at large in the country, to lose no time in properly organising, so as to be ready when Mr Montagu comes here, to place the real situation before him, and to be able to do so we must set to work at once.

DANGER FROM INTERESTED PARTIES.

I notice that already interested parties are setting up people against the Home Rule League, which is being misrepresented as going beyond the demand of the Congress and the League. As President of the Bombay Home Rule League I can but repeat that all that we want is, and all that the entire organization of ours is devoted to, is the realization of the scheme of reforms adopted at Lucknow, with this difference, that the Home Rule League is an educationist propaganda and the Congress is a mere deliberative body, I feel sure that the Mussalmans and the Hindus will stand together on this matter, and I trust that whatever intrigues might be set up by interested parties to detach any section of the landed aristocracy or the Hindus or Mahomedans is doomed to failure.

QUESTION OF NATIVE STATES.

Personally, I appreciate fully some of the questions affecting the Ruling Chiefs of India, and I am sure that they feel for India as much as any one of us, as was clearly demonstrated by the speeches at the historic send-off that was given to the Maharaja of Bikanir at Bombay by the ruling chiefs, prior to his departure to England as a representative at the Imperial War Conference. But the question of British India and its administration should not be allowed to be mixed up with that of the Native States."

THE ANGLO-INDIAN AGITATION
NOVEMBER, 1917

A representative of the Associated Press asked Mr. Jinnah what he thought of the attitude recently taken up by the European commercial community on the present political situation. In reply, Mr. Jinnah said :—

Their attitude with reference to the policy declared by His Majesty's Government through Mr. Montagu, Secretary of State for India, and the speech of H. E. the Viceroy in the Council on 5th September and subsequent release of Mrs Besant and her colleagues, is wanting in foresight and judgment. In his opinion Government have shown the greatest wisdom in recognising the needs of the situation. It is a sign of strength in any Government to recognise the claims of justice, human freedom and public opinion. In releasing Mrs. Besant and others Government had recognised and followed those principles. "I am sure," Mr. Jinnah asserted, "thinking India heartily appreciates this policy, I feel confident that the appeal of the Viceroy has evoked the warmest response. On our side we shall faithfully adhere to the truce. From what I know of the Government of India individually and collectively I feel certain that they are willing to give us full, patient and considerate hearing. A constitution which will bring freedom to India must be framed. Freedom, which in its political aspect is responsible Government, is a human and not western ideal. A responsible Government has a perfectly definite meaning. It implies an executive removable at the will of an elected legislature or by the electorate. Responsible Government is the goal of British policy in India and that is our goal.

NO CONSTRUCTIVE PROPOSALS PUT FORTH.

The European commercial community has offered no constructive suggestions on their part. Theirs has been merely a destructive criticism and an obstructive attitude which will not do. I may say that the days of the Ilbert Bill opposition have gone. I have tried to understand what the grievances of the European commercial community are. In the mass of platitudes and generalities one argument which is brought out, though not quite definitely, is about the security of British capital in India. British capital has been sunk in Mysore before the rendition, but the province was handed over none the less to the former ruling family, and since more British capital, I believe, is sunk in Mysore. According to figures available up to 1915 I find the British capital in India is about £400 millions in South Africa about £400 millions, in Canada and Newfoundland about £600 millions, in Australia £450 millions. We know these investments in British colonies did not stand in the way of their getting self-government. Why should British investments of much smaller amount prevent India from receiving her birthright? Besides, British investments in foreign countries amount to about £2,000 millions, to say nothing of the loans or advances to foreign countries and allies. Is the Republic of Argentine under British rule, where I believe no less than £350 millions of British capital has been invested, to say nothing of China and Persia where millions have been invested? I was not a little amused that a shrewd business man like Mr. Wardlaw Milne, Chairman of the European Association meeting of Bombay, should have indulged in platitudes which show how thoroughly he is engrossed in making money in India and how little he knows of the present political situation in the country. He thinks any stick is now good enough to beat the so-called extremists and thus put down the demand of India. This is what he said:—"Under no consideration the European community in India will allow itself to be menaced and its voice unheard." Whoever suggested such a proposition? Our battle-cry has been that in our own country we must be treated as the King's equal subjects. He says, at another place. "We realise progress must be made. We are not opposed to it. On the contrary we welcome it. We believe that the greater portion of the Indian people hold views in no way at variance with those we hold, and that they are to a large extent opposed to the extremists section."

Do the 19 members of the Imperial Council who submitted the memorandum a year ago belong to the extremist section? Does Mr. Milne think that the representative committees appointed by the Indian National Congress and the All-India Moslem League to frame a scheme of reforms belong to the extremist section? Does Mr. Milne think that the united voice of the Congress and the Moslem League at Lucknow was that of a small extremist section?

OUT OF TOUCH WITH PUBLIC OPINION.

Observations of this character show how little the non-official Europeans are in touch with public opinion in India. However, I would urge upon my countrymen not to minimise this opposition, vague as it is. We must take measures to face it and remove the misrepresentations that might influence the British public and Parliament. I think nothing of the European commercial community opposition till they come out with a definite scheme of reforms which they say "they welcome." What are the "constitutional," "gradual" and "reasonable" reforms? I am sure that a man of the calibre and statesmanship of Mr. Montagu would like less of such platitudes and generalities and would like to know more what are the definite proposals of those "Sons of the Empire," who in India say "India for the Empire and the Empire for India," though we hear a different doctrine preached in the colonies.

THE NEW UNITY.

In very eloquent appreciation of the work of the president of the Conference, Mr. Jinnah made some observations which are worthy of note:—

When the late Sir Syed Ahmed said thirty years ago that the Hindus and Mahomedans were like the two eyes of a beautiful damsel and that injury to the one hurt the other, he indicated a passive stage of national life when Hindus and Mahomedans contented themselves with the formula of not hurting each other. "We have now reached the active stage," said Mr. Jinnah, "when we realise that we must co-operate with one another for national work. Ahmedabad, he also said, had given birth to re-union. Henceforth there would be no extremists or moderates—but all true nationalists"—who would constantly endeavour by all constitutional means to attain the goal and would not go to sleep. For, "our souls have been roused. We are in earnest."

ELEMENTARY EDUCATION BILL.

In supporting Mr. Gokhale's Elementary Education Bill at the Imperial Legislative Council (April, 1912), Mr. Jinnah spoke as follows:—

"Sir, I do not think that anybody in this Council can deny the paramount importance of this measure. It has been said that this Bill is going to be thrown out. It is very often said in this Council that, unless Government are willing to accept any Resolution or any measure, it cannot be passed in this Council. Now I for one do not wish in any way to taunt Government in this matter. The Council, as it is constituted now, we know perfectly well that the intention is not that in this Council we can defeat the Government and replace the Government bench by the people of this country, by non-official members. Council, as it is constituted now, it is well understood that it is impossible to appeal to the Council and ask them to vote on any Resolution or measure according to their own convictions; but the sole function to which the non-official members —a minority—are reduced in this Council is only to express their views on all questions that come before this Council. That being the sole function to which I am reduced here, I think that on an important measure of this character I should not give my silent vote, but should express my views and give my reasons in support of this Bill. I regret very much that some of my countrymen are opposed to this Bill. Well, Sir, it is our misfortune that there should be this difference of opinion. One thing I can assure this Council of, and that is this, that great and overwhelming majority of my people are with me. When I was speaking on the Marriage Bill the other day, I frankly and openly admitted that I was supporting a minority, that the majority of my people were opposed to that measure. But my innermost convictions were in favour of that measure, and I felt it my duty to support the motion. In the same spirit I ask those who are opposed to this Bill to concede to me that great majority of my countrymen, Hindus and Mussalmans, are in favour of and support the Bill. That being so, Sir, I have a double satisfaction: not only my innermost convictions are in favour of this Bill, which shall always be the first and foremost consideration with me either in opposing or supporting a measure, but I have the additional happiness that even the opinion of my countrymen, of the majority of them, is in favour of it. Sir, a very great deal has been said about the merits of this Bill. The Hon'ble Mr. Gokhale—whom, if I may, I take the liberty of congratulating for the able and masterly way in which he has dealt with this question, and for the services that he has rendered to the country, and I only pray that India may have many more sons like him—has laid down here clearly that the cardinal principle of this Bill is the introduction of compulsion in selected areas. To that what is the answer of the Government? The Hon'ble Sir Harcourt Butler, whose reply was not very pleasing to me, but at the same time it was not very displeasing—it was what I would call middling—the Hon'ble Sir Harcourt Butler said that as to the ends that we have in view, we are at one, but only we differ as to the means and the ways. And the Hon'ble Sir Harcourt Butler said that to Government it seems that the best way and means to achieve that end which we all desire, namely, to kill the enemy of ignorance, would be the extension, the gradual extension, with a little more speed than we have been going for the last 150 years, namely, the gradual extension of the principle of the voluntary system. Well, Sir, the real issue therefore—and I wish to draw the attention of the Council to the real issues: I do not wish to deal with individual members—that you have got before the Council to-day is this: is this the method which the Government suggest the best method, is that the proper method or not? Now, Sir, my answer is this, and I think it will be conceded in this Council in all fairness, and it has been conceded outside this Council in all fairness, that one of the greatest reproaches against the British rule is the neglect of elementary education in this country. We have been under the British rule for the last 150 years, and, Sir, the figures that the Hon'ble Mr. Gokhale has given to this Council more than once show in what condition, in what state, the elementary education of the country at present is. We have been trying this system, namely, the principle of the extension of the voluntary system, for the last 50 years or 60 years seriously, and we know what has been the result. In one word, in one sentence, if I may say so, you are going at a jog-trot pace, and that jog-trot pace we object to. By this method you have shown conclusively, and the Hon'ble Mr. Gokhale has shown conclusively by figures, that it will take 175 years in order to get all the school-going age children to school, and 600 years to get all the girls to school. I do not wish to be misunderstood here for a single moment. I do not wish to minimise the efforts of the Government. I fully recognize that within the last few years the Education Member full-fledged sitting there now, was created before many of us expected that happy state of things in this Council. I do not dispute, Sir, that efforts have been made. The announcement by our King-Emperor of the grant of 50 lakhs of rupees for elementary education at the Delhi Durbar was more welcome. If I may say so with great deference these accelerated methods which have been adopted have come into force recently and are largely due to no little spur from the non-official criticism for which the Hon'ble Mr. Gokhale deserves all credit. But once this measure is rejected, once we are relegated to the principle of voluntary system, I have no doubt the Government will do all they can, but it will not be the same as having the principle of compulsion introduced in this country. Therefore I say, Sir, that the question is this. We are not satisfied that the methods and ways that you suggest are the best. We are convinced that the progress will be inordinately slow, and we are convinced that there is no salvation for the masses unless the principle of compulsion is introduced into this country. In no country has elementary education become universal without compulsion. But the answer of the Hon'ble Sir Harcourt Butler is, the time has not come (of course he does not indicate when the time will come, that is left in obscurity› for which he deserves great credit), he says, first of all, you cannot compare India with other countries of the world. I admit that the conditions of India are in certain respects different from the conditions of other countries of the world. But I think even the Hon'ble Sir Harcourt Butler will admit that the people of India, if I may say so, belong to the same species, namely, human beings; in that respect I think we resemble all other nations of the world, and all other countries. And if the conditions of India are different, which I concede to a certain extent, surely therein comes the statesman, therein comes the politician: it is his business to meet those special conditions, and to provide safeguards which are necessary. It is no use saying India is different. India has got a number of languages, a number of castes, a number of creeds. What has this got to do with the number of castes, religions and creeds? We have no doubt to take these conditions into consideration and provide for them, and I appeal to the statesman. Then the Hon'ble Sir Harcourt Butler gave certain figures. I am not dealing with the case of England or the Philippine Islands. He dealt with the case of Ceylon, Baroda and other places. Well, I understand that some of the figures which Sir Harcourt Butler gave us are not quite correct ; but as the Hon'ble Mr. Gokhale is a specialist in statistics and figures, I propose to leave it to him when he comes to deal with the Hon'ble Sir Harcourt Butler in reply. All I say is that the figures are not, as I understand, correct. Then, Sir, the next point which Sir Harcourt Butler took was that there were not enough school buildings and there were not sufficient teachers. Well, Sir, I submit there is not much force in that argument. The real force in the argument is, whether you have got money or not. If you have money, you will get teachers ; if you have money, you will get school buildings. The real point is whether you have got money or not. Therefore, Sir, if I am right to this extent that your method, namely, the gradual extension of the principle of voluntary system, is not good, does not and will not produce the results desired, is too slow for the progress of the country, and if our method is right, namely, the system of compulsion in selected areas, then once you assume that we are right, we shall at once be faced with the second question, where is the money and how are we to do it? I attach no importance, Sir, with very great respect to the argument of Sir Harcourt Butler that you cannot get teachers and school buildings, if you have money, I say you can get them, with really little or no difficulty, only you may have to wait a little; but I say it is not an insurmountable difficulty. Therefore, Sir, the next question I wish to answer is the question of finance. Now, Sir, this is a very very old story that you have no money, and all I can say is this, find money! Find money!! Find money!!! I appeal to the President—find money I appeal to the President not as President, but as the Finance Minister. I say, find money. If you say you have not got enough money, discover and tap new sources of taxation. But, Sir, what is the provision of this Bill? Before I go into that wider question of finding money, what is the provision of this Bill? The provision, as far as

I understand, is this. First of all, you have to comply with what I would call the condition precedent, and the condition precedent is that unless in a particular area you have 33 per cent. or whatever figure may be hereafter fixed under the rules to be made by the Governor-General in Council under this Bill—but I will take the figure of the Hon'ble Mr. Gokhale, 33 per cent.—first of all, unless you have 33 per cent. of school-going age boys at school, no local body will be in a position to apply to extend or enforce the provisions of this Bill to that particular area. Now, Sir, as the Hon'ble, Mr. Gokhale has pointed out, it will cost roughly about 3 crores of rupees to the Imperial Exchequer. The total cost will be 4½ crores, one-third to be paid by the local bodies, because it is only on that condition they can introduce the operation of this Bill into that particular area. On the other hand, the Hon'ble Sir Harcourt Butler says it will be double. He has not given us his reasons for it or data, but has simply stated that it will be double. The Hon'ble Mr. Gokhale has given his reasons and data for his figures, and therefore with very very great respect I must say that I prefer reasons to mere assertions, and I say that, until I am convinced to the contrary, which I am not, I will take the figure of the Hon'ble Mr. Gokhale—3 crores—to be correct. Now, Sir, I ask, is it such an insurmountable difficulty to get 3 crores of rupees from the Imperial Exchequer? Is it such a great, gigantic feat to be performed for a country like India with its 300 millions of people? I say, Sir, that there is nothing in that argument. I ask the Government; I say 'find the money; if necessary, tax the people.' But I shall be told that the people are already taxed; I shall be told that we shall be facing great unpopularity; and I shall be told, why should we do all this? My answer is that we should do all this to improve the masses of this country to whom you owe a much greater duty than to anybody else. My answer is that you must remove that reproach that is levelled justly against British rule, namely, the neglect of elementary education. My answer is that it is the duty of every civilized Government to educate masses, and if you have to face unpopularity, if you have to face a certain amount of danger, face it boldly in the name of duty; and I say it in this Council here without hesitation that you will have the whole educated public with you in the struggle on the battle-field. Therefore, fear not: do not listen to the alarmist that you will make yourself unpopular if you advocate and fight the cause of elementary education.

"Now, the next point which I shall deal with in the speech of the Hon'ble Sir Harcourt Butler is this. He said that the Local Governments who have expressed their opinions and who are supposed to know the local conditions of the country have almost every one of them opposed this Bill. The Local Governments have given various reasons for opposing this measure. He only said that the Local Governments are opposed to this measure. He did not tell us which of the arguments, which of the objections of the Local Governments, he thought were sound arguments and objections of weight. But, Sir, I had an opportunity of going through this file as much as I possibly could. I find the Local Governments, as far as I can understand, have opposed this Bill, first, on the ground of political danger. This also includes a small non-official public who oppose this Bill. Secondly, that the voluntary system of extending primary education is better; and thirdly, have hinted in some places of social danger; and fourthly, taxation and the cost. I have already dealt with the question of cost and I cannot say anything more. I am not in charge of the Finance portfolio and I am not on the Government Bench. Otherwise I should certainly occupy myself in finding ways and means of financing this measure. I have dealt with the costs; I have dealt with the issue which really is the issue, namely, whether the voluntary system is better or whether compulsion is better. There are therefore only two other points, namely, the political danger and the social danger. Now, the social danger has not been advocated in this Council except by one or two members. My friend the Hon'ble Nawab Abdul Majid has said that there will be strikes and there will be Socialists amongst us, and I think the Hon'ble Nawab Majid brought in the political danger that if you give education they will become agitators. Well, Sir, I honestly and sincerely appeal to the Government: do you really think that education means sedition? I say, Sir, that a frank and independent criticism of the Government or the measures of Government is the duty of every member of the State. But let me tell you that you have no better friends in this country—I mean the friends of the Government—than the educated classes of this country. But, if I may say so, we love the British Government, but we love our country more. We come forward and criticise the Government. We say 'you are going wrong. It may be we are wrong; it does not follow because we say you are wrong therefore you are wrong.' But surely fair, free and independent criticisms of the acts of Government, of the measures of Government do not constitute sedition. Therefore, I say, Sir, can you argue seriously that education means sedition? Do you mean that if you can get a boy who can read and write a little that he will become a political agitator? Can you seriously believe that? On the other hand, however, we know the blessings of education. We have learnt that from the British Government. They have been the first to open our eyes to it. They have brought us up to this level when we can stand in this Council and deliberate upon the affairs of our nation and of our country. I ask, Sir, where would the Hon'ble Nawab Majid be but for his education? I ask, Sir, where would the Hon'ble Muhammad Shafi be (he is not here I see) but for his education? Therefore, Sir, it cannot be denied as to the boon that education brings to the country. Then it is said 'Oh! but the people will become too big for their boots', if I may use that expression, that 'they will not follow the occupation of their parents, they will demand more rights, there will be strikes, they will become Socialists.' Well, Sir, are you going to keep millions and millions of people trodden under your feet for fear that they may demand more rights; are you going to keep them in ignorance and darkness for ever and for all ages to come because they may stand up against you and say that we have certain rights and you must give them to us? Is that the feeling of humanity? Is that the spirit of humanity? I say, Sir, that it is the duty of the zamindars and of the landlords to be a little less selfish. I say, Sir, that it is the duty of the educated classes to be a little less selfish. They must not monopolise the pedestals, but they must be prepared to meet their people. They must be prepared to be brought down from their pedestals if they do not do their duties properly. I say, Sir, that it is the elementary right of every man to say if he is wronged that he is wronged and that he should be righted. I say, Sir, there is nothing in that argument. It may be that in England and other countries in certain circles it has been urged that this elementary education has been a mistake. But by whom is this urged? Not by those who have benefited by it but by those who have been influenced by selfish reasons because they have suffered. It is this class which says that it has been a mistake to have introduced universal elementary education

"Therefore, Sir, I say there is nothing so far

as the social danger is concerned, I say there is nothing so far as the political danger is concerned. You will have greater friends, you will have more intelligent friends who will understand you better and so your work will be all the more easy. You will have less unscrupulous people who are at present in a position to impose upon the ignorant and who are in a position to rile them against you when there is no cause, when there is no reason but for purposes of their own. Therefore I say, Sir, I have not the slightest hesitation in saying, that I am convinced that the method advocated by the Hon'ble Mr. Gokhale is the best method in the interests of our country.

"There is one word more, Sir, before I finish. I do not think it is necessary to mention these things really, but one is forced into this lest one may be misunderstood. But for the present state of the Mussalman community and in some quarters in particular, I do not think it is necessary for any Mussalman to say that he would not do anything either in this Council or outside this Council which is likely to prejudice the interest or the cause of his community. I, Sir, yield to none in that respect. If this Bill had been referred to the Select Committee as I wish it, if certain requirements were not embodied in this Bill by the Select Committee to safeguard the Mussalmans, and if this Bill would have come before this Council without those requirements, which I think will be necessary in the interest of the Muhammadans in the present state of the condition of the people in this country, I would have been the first to oppose that Bill until and unless those requirements were incorporated in the Bill. But that is not the question, that is not the point, before the Council to-day. Therefore, I will only rest content by saying this that if this Bill were referred to the Select Committee, and if this Bill did not provide for certain requirements and modifications which I think are just in the interests of the Mussalmans, I would certainly then be the first to oppose it. But the present state of this Bill is a motion to refer it to the Select Committee, and that motion I have no hesitation in supporting."

THE MUSSALMAN WAKF VALIDATING BILL

At the Imperial Legislative Council (April, 1913) in moving the report of the Select Committee on the above bill the Hon. Mr. Jinnah said:—

Sir,—I move that the Report of the Select Committee on the Bill to declare the rights of Mussalmans to make settlements of property by way of wakf in favour of their families, children and descendants, be taken into consideration.

In moving this, Sir, I have only got to deal with a very few points, and all that I have to say is with regard to the objections that have been raised by the different provinces, particularly the High Court Judges, the District Judges and non-Mussalman opinion. The one objection which has been urged against the Bill is the question of public policy. Now the answer to that, Sir, is a very simple one, and, as I have already explained in my speech when I introduced the Bill, what we have got to do is to administer the Muhammadan Law to the Mussalmans, and therefore to introduce the question of public policy which is foreign to the Islamic jurisprudence, to my mind is outside the question, and there is no such thing as public policy of any kind, so far as Muhammadan jurisprudence is concerned, to which the provisions of this Bill are in any way opposed. I therefore give that simple answer to that point.

Another point was that we must protect the creditors, and with regard to that, as the Council knows, the Bill, as it was originally introduced, contained certain clauses, which were intended to prevent fraud against creditors. Those clauses, when they came to be considered in a Select Committee, we, on careful consideration, found it very difficult to maintain without in any way infringing upon the personal law that governs the Mussalmans in this country. That being so, it was after very careful consideration, decided by the Select Committee unanimously that the registration clauses should be dropped.

But so far as this point is concerned and this is the second point and the only point really with which we are concerned—and the criticisms are concerned, it seems to me, Sir, that the Muhammadan Law, as it stands to-day, provides certain safeguards against fraud upon creditors. The fraud upon creditors may be divided into two parts: first, a fraud which may be practised when the wakf is created; so far as that part of the law is concerned, there are safeguards, as I said already, in the Muhammadan Law. Then with regard to the frauds which may be practised upon the creditors after the wakf has been actually created, it seems to me that we have got already the Registration Act, which lays down that every wakf that is made in writing must be registered, and that notice by virtue of its being registered is a sufficient safeguard to that extent. No doubt a Muhammadan may make an oral wakf, and in that case it may prejudice the creditor to a certain extent. The answer to that is, that that is Mussalman Law and you cannot override the Mussalman law. If you compel the Mussalman to make wakf in writing and in no other manner, you are, to that extent, overriding the Mussalman law, and therefore I for one am not prepared to accept any provision which is in any way likely to overrule or affect the personal law of the Mussalmans. A man stands in a very serious position indeed if he makes an oral wakf when he comes to prove it in a Court of Law, and therefore now-a-days people do not make oral wakfs. Thus the very apprehended fear is so very small, whereas, in order to rectify the fear, the danger of infringing upon the Mussalman law is so great, and taking the two considerations, the one overbalances the other to such an extent that I felt that I could not possibly have that provision.

One word more, Sir, and I have done; and that is this—that my Hindu friends must remember that although one of these provisions, *viz.*, the last provision which I have mentioned, the regulating of oral wakfs, is the only danger so far as I can see. With regard to that, my Hindu friends must also understand this, that it affects the Mussalmans to a much greater extent, it prejudices them to a much greater extent than it would the creditors who may happen to be Hindus; for this reason, that it will depreciate the Mussalman's title to the property to a great extent. Therefore, remember, Sir, that is not being able to accept this provision or this suggestion, *viz*, to prevent the Mussalmans from making oral wakfs, the fear being very small, I am not only guided by this fact, that my Hindu friends will suffer, but the Mussalmans will equally suffer: if not more, therefore, we would certainly like, if we could possibly do it, to have this provision in our own interest because otherwise it certainly depreciates the title to movable property so far as the Mussalmans in this country are concerned. Therefore my Hindu friends will, I know, sympathise with me that I am tied down by my law to such an extent, that, although to a certain extent, that I am unable to alter it. And the position of the Government is still more difficult because by their charter they have undertaken and pledged themselves to administer the Mussalman Law to the Mussalmans and the Hindu law to the Hindus, and therefore, these being the difficulties in our way, we had eventually to abandon the registration clauses With these remarks, I hope and am confident the Council will pass this Bill unanimously. I will only say one word more, Sir, and that is this : I wish on my own behalf and on behalf of the Muhammadans of India to express our sincere gratitude to His Excellency the Viceroy and his Government for the manner in which they have received and treated the Bill in this Council.

It has made us feel that the Government in this matter has acted as if it was our Government in every sense of the word. Their spirit, their feeling, their help have enabled me to pilot this Bill through the Council. I trust the Government will always make us feel that it is our Government and if we have got a reasonable complaint, a reasonable grievance to put before you fairly and properly, you will meet us fairly and properly ; and I trust that in other matters that may come hereafter before this Council or outside this Council, the Government will extend the same spirit and the same attitude towards us.

After long discussion in the Council on the adoption of the bill, Mr. Jinnah spoke as under in conclusion:—

Sir, first of all, I must thank Hon'ble Members who have spoken of me in very kind terms, and I also thank the Government and the Hon'ble Law Member who has expressed his kind feelings towards such work as I may have done in this matter: but I specially and particularly welcome the congratulation from my old and revered friend, the Hon'ble Babu Surendranath Banerjee, who represents a volume of opinion in Bengal, and, coming from him as a Hindu, I particularly appreciate it and I wish to thank him very much for it. With regard to his support, I feel most grateful to him.

With regard to the Hon'ble Mr. Vijiaraghavachariar, I must say that the Hon'ble Member to-day happens to be in a mood of opposition. While opposing the provision of the Bill, the Hon'ble Member was good enough to wind up by supporting it. While finding fault with the provisions of the Bill and saying that the Mussalmans are getting a law which is going to give them a system of primogeniture, he supported it. I now appeal to the Hon'ble Member; his suggestion was that we want to do these things under the guise of the fiction of Mussalman law, we do not want to face the Privy Council; although we have got there the Right Hon'ble Mr. Amir Ali, we are afraid to face the Privy Council because of the English Judges. Really I appeal to the Hon'ble Member and his experience. He knows perfectly well that never in the history of the Privy Council has that tribunal ever revised its judgment And, Sir, is it right for a lawyer of his experience to tell me why is it that I do not go to that tribunal which has already decided this point and ask for a revision?

"Then the Hon'ble Member criticised very firmly and said that this Bill was not the Mussalman law, that the Privy Council's decision was the Mussalman law. Well, with very great respect for him, he is entitled to his opinion. Every man is entitled to his opinion. With very great deference, I may point out to him that the highest authorities, Mussalman and English Jurists of eminence, have declared with the utmost deference for that great tribunal, the Privy Council, that their decision is not in accordance with Mussalman law. The whole of my community, with a few exceptions—for whom, also, I have respect, because each man is entitled to his own opinion—are of opinion that the Privy Council's decision is not correct exposition of the Mussalman law. Therefore, Sir, our only remedy was to appeal to the Government, appeal to the legislature, and the Government have come to our rescue. That ought not to excite any jealousy; that ought not to excite any envy of any kind whatever, that ought not to entitle any one to say that by these circuitous methods we get a system of law, namely primogeniture, and not Mussalman law.

"However, I do not wish, Sir, to go into these details because the Hon'ble Member has given me his support. I appreciate the support he has given, no matter the manner in which he has given it. Then he says with regard to clause 3, how does that clause come in at all? I have explained to the Hon'ble Member myself, and if he looks up any textbook on Muhammadan law, he will find that what is reproduced in clause 3 is nothing but Muhammadan law, namely, that one of the purposes recognised by Mussalman law as purposes for which you can make a wakf as if a man happens to be Hunufia for his own support, maintenance or payment of debts—that is a purpose for which he can make a wakf, and the Privy Council's decision was that if you postpone the dedication to charity for a certain period—and if the dedication to charity is proposed to be given at any period too remote—then that wakf is invalid. Therefore if a Hunufia Mussalman makes a wakf for payment of his debts, and if this clause is not inserted, the Privy Council's decision will stand and you have only got to take it to any Court of Law to set aside the wakf. Therefore, it is absolutely essential that this purpose, which was so to say overridden by the decision of the Privy Council, must be specifically mentioned in the clause to show that it is a purpose for which you can make a wakf. Then the last point was the point about creditors. Well I have already told the Council as to what the position is. The Hon'ble Mr. Sitanath Roy Rai Bahadur had amendments about this on the Agenda List which he was good enough to withdraw. Now I can only assure the Hon'ble Member that so far as the first amendment is concerned, I have not the slightest doubt in my own mind, and I appeal to any lawyer, that secured creditors cannot be affected by the making of a wakf after the security is given. The only question, as I pointed out, is the question of unsecured creditors, and if a man while he is making his wakf is in an insolvent condition, and he makes his wakf in order to defraud, defeat or delay his creditors, then I say without any hesitation that that wakf will be set aside by any Court of Law under Muhammadan law. If you can prove that the wakf is created in order to defeat the creditors, or defraud the creditors, or delay the creditors, you have only got to prove that and the wakf will be set aside. There is the Provisional Insolvency Act and there is the Presidency Towns Insolvency Act. If a man in any way goes against those provisions, the Court of

Bankruptcy will set aside his wakf. But the difficulty that does arise—and I do recognise that there is difficulty—and that is in the case of testamentary wakf or an oral wakf, that is to say, the wakf may have been made when the man was in a perfectly solvent state and not intended to defeat, defraud or delay his creditors; but an oral wakf perfectly good at the time it was made. His heirs may suppress the fact of any wakf having been made and dispose of the property as they like. A second or third generation may come up and attempt to prove that an oral wakf had been made. I say if a man comes to a Court of Law after one or two generations and attempts to prove an oral wakf, I appeal to you—not as lawyers but as men of common sense—what Court of Law would accept such proof; and the consequence will be that he will never succeed in proving the wakf. But that small danger is there, and the danger affects Mussalmans a great deal more than any other community.

It affects Europeans, but Europeans as a rule do not purchase or deal with immovable property. That danger is there, and very small danger though it be it affects us much more seriously than other communities, because, as the Hon'ble Member admitted very frankly, it depreciates the title to Mussalman property. Our difficulty is how are we to override the provision of Muhammadan law which empowers a Mussalman to make an oral wakf. We are unable to do it, and therefore what little apprehension there may be among the other communities I ask them to that extent to bear with us who are suffering along with the others to a much greater extent. One word more and I have done. Before I sit down I wish to offer my personal thanks to the Hon'ble the Law Member for the most able and valuable help he gave me in the Select Committee to get this Bill through, and in that I include our able Secretary, Sir William Vincent, who gave us equally valuable help in the matter before the Select Committee, after the Select Committee and during the Select Committee.

THE INDIAN CRIMINAL LAW AMENDMENT BILL.

The following is the text of the Speech of the Hon'ble Mr. Jinnah in the Imperial Legislative Council, April 1913, on the Indian Criminal Law Amendment Bill.

SIR,—I want first of all to put it before the Council very clearly that nobody more readily would respond to that appeal that has come from the Hon'ble Home Member than I would, also I wish to express that nobody condemns in stronger terms the misdeeds of which a long list was given to us a few minutes ago by the Home Member. I also wish to express that every attempt on the part of my countrymen to undermine the authority of the Government and to disturb the law and order in my opinion deserves the strongest condemnation and the highest punishment. Those men who have a desire to undermine the authority of the Government; those men who have a desire to disturb the law and order, are in my opinion the biggest enemies of my country and my people. They are to-day doing the greatest harm to the cause of India. Sir, why is this measure brought before this Council to-day? It is brought because of the doings of some of my countrymen. Repressive measures that have been brought in, in this Council have been brought because of the misdeeds of some of our countrymen. I remember, Sir, in 1910, when the Press Bill was introduced at Calcutta, much as we felt that a severe blow was going to be dealt at the liberty of the Press, much as we felt that our most prized liberty, namely, the liberty of the Press was going to be curtailed, our hands were tied, our mouths were closed by the misdeeds of some of the misguided men who belong to our country, and we almost, as a body of non-official members, realised and felt that the Government were bound to take certain measures to maintain order and law: and reluctant as we were, we felt that, although we were losing what we prized most, namely, the liberty of the Press to a certain extent, we not only supported it, but we supported it with every power that was in our possession.

Sir, I believe in criticising Government, I believe in criticising Government freely and frankly, but at the same time that it is the duty of every educated man to support and help the Government when the Government is right. On this occasion I feel that having regard to the history of political crimes, my hands are tied, my mouth is closed and my countrymen who are responsible for these deeds are responsible to-day for my position which I occupy in this Council at this moment. Let those men who still have these misguided ideas, let those men who have these hallucinations, realise that, by anarchism, by dastardly crimes, they cannot bring about good Government, let them yet realise that those methods have not succeeded in any country in the world, and are not likely to succeed in India. Let those men yet realise before it is too late, and before they bring their country into a position which may be more regretted by every patriot who feels for and loves his Motherland: let them yet realise that those are not the methods. Sir, if I may say so, I represent a class, an educated class and young

India in this country. Representing the modern India and the young educated class in this country, I feel that I am expressing their sentiments on this occasion and I feel that there is a large body of men who feel exactly as I am feeling to-day. The Hon'ble the Home Member said, 'we have got cause, we have considered our position, and we ask the Council to take us on trust and support Government.' Having regard to the position that I have described, I have no alternative, Sir, but to take the Government on trust on this occasion. I, therefore, think, Sir, that so far as the principle of this Bill is concerned, I am not in a position to resist it. With regard to the merits of this Bill, I wish, Sir, to make certain observations. This Bill, as the Hon'ble Home Member said, is nothing but the English Law. I beg to take the opportunity of pointing out to the Hon'ble Member few things especially for him to consider, and I have no doubt that in Select Committee, the members who will be on the Select Committee, will consider the few suggestions that I wish to make to-day. I shall not be here any more in this Council, therefore I shall not be able to take any part in the various stages through which this Bill will go: and therefore I draw the most earnest attention of the Hon'ble the Home Member and the members who are on the Select Committee to consider those suggestions that I shall make. The first suggestion that I wish to make, and which is an obvious error, that occurs often. It is made, not only in this case, but speaking from experience, in several cases when you come to enact a statute following or copying English statute or law which is distributed in and covered by different statutes or branches of law. You have to be most careful when you are copying English law as you propose to do in the present case. Sometimes you come to enact a statute and you are dealing with substantive law, but along with the substantive law you have the Law of procedure or evidence, and while you are rectifying or amending or enacting the substantive law, you lose sight of the law, of procedure or evidence, and when it comes to be worked actually in a court of law, there is almost an impasse, and the result is almost startling. A very recent case from that point of view arose in Bombay with regard to the Indian Companies Law that will perhaps interest the Hon'ble Member in charge of the commercial portfolio. It was with regard to the position of the secured creditor, whether he should be allowed to prove for the full amount of his claim or debt or not. The English Companies Act of 1862 was enacted and afterwards there came the Judicature Act 1875, which altered the position of the secured creditor. But when we came to enact our law of 1866, the Indian Companies Act, we took it boldly from the English Act, having lost sight of the Judicature Act of 1875, and when we came to amend it in 1882, we were still asleep, having lost sight of the Judicature Act of 1875 again, and we only woke up when the present Bill which is pending came up before the Council the other day and that was because when the English Consolidated Act came into force in 1908, the section in the Judicature Act was incorporated in substance in the English Act. Therefore,

Sir, with regard to this Bill now, I point out the provisions embodied in Section 10 of the Indian Evidence Act which have most important bearings on the Bill under discussion.

The substantive law is laid down in clause 120A. That any agreement between two or more persons to do or cause to be done an illegal act, that agreement *per se* is a conspiracy; or an act which is not illegal but by illegal means such an agreement is designated as criminal conspiracy. When you come to consider the rule of evidence in India, section 10 of the Evidence Act is a most important section to bear in mind, because in the English law of evidence as laid down, you will find it different. It lays down clearly that no evidence is admissible to prove the offence against the accused, unless some act, omission or declaration, something done or written by one or other of the conspirators was done in furtherance of the common object or purpose, *viz.*, 'conspiracy.' 'In *furtherance*'—those are the words to which I wish to draw the attention of the Hon'ble Member; whereas in the Indian Evidence Act you will find that the words are '*in reference*' instead of '*in furtherance*'. Now clearly you are changing the substantive law in India and bringing it into line with the English law. But it will have the Indian Law of Evidence untouched, and I submit it will lead to very great hardship and danger. Remember, that when you are enacting a penal statute your object is to arrest the evil—your object is to punish the guilty. But, Sir, legislating as we are doing in this Council for 300 millions of people, you must not forget your responsibility to the innocent and law-abiding subjects of His Majesty. Such cases have the greatest claim to your consideration. Therefore I say, while you are bringing this law into line with the English law, follow it strictly in all its bearings. I will only refer to that section 10. Just to show that—it says this:

'*Where there is reasonable ground* to believe that two or more persons have conspired together to commit offences &c. anything said, done or written by any one of such persons *in reference* to their common intention at the time when such intention was first entertained by any one of them is a relevant fact as against each of the persons believed to be so conspiring as well for the purpose of proving the existence of the conspiracy, as for the purpose of showing that any such person was a party to it.'

The Hon'ble the Home Member has pointed out, and very rightly pointed out, conspiracy in India *per se* is not an offence except under section 121 A, and therefore unless something was done in furtherance of the common intention it was not an offence. But this Bill now goes much further. Now, Sir, the English Law of Evidence in cases of conspiracy to which I would like to draw the attention of the Hon'ble Member is laid down in Taylor on Evidence. I give a reference to paragraphs 590, 591 and 593 There you will find,—I do not wish to weary the Council because really this is highly a technical subject, and I dare say it is not very interesting to most of you here; but I only wish to draw the attention of the Hon'ble Member that there, he will find, very clearly laid down that any act, omission or declaration or something said, done or written by one of the conspirators, before it can be admitted as evidence against the accused conspirator it must be in furtherance of the conspiracy.

Then there is another point to which I wish to draw the attention of the Hon'ble Member. It is this: the explanation to clause 120 A. of the Bill seems to me to go much beyond the English law, and is likely to create mischief when you come to interpret that clause. I entirely agree with the Hon'ble Member that without this explanation the law as reproduced in clause 120 A, is substantially the English law; but the explanation in my opinion goes a little further, and it might and well, I think, create the greatest mischief if left as it stands now, and I am of opinion that this explanation should be dropped. Then the third point is with regard to how the prosecution should be launched. Remember, if you pass this Bill you are really making conspiracy an offence, although it may not be an offence against the Government, the State or the King, in the sense, namely, of undermining Government or the authority of Government and therefore you are going much beyond those offences which are known as offences against the state or Government. A criminal breach of trust or theft, and many other offences are covered by this Bill. If A and B agree to commit a theft in the house of X, the moment they agree to do that and nothing more by way of overt act, and if you can prove they agreed, then simply because there happen to be two or more persons who agreed to that effect is conspiracy and an offence and they are certainly punishable by this Bill. Therefore you are going far beyond your purpose, which is to punish offences against the state or Government. I take it that the main object of this Bill is really to reach those cases which are strictly speaking offences against the state, and the act ought to be restricted to those offences. You will find the practice in England in such cases laid down in Halsbury's Laws of England. I am reading from the 'Laws of England' Volume X, page 292, paragraph 602, which says it is the duty of the Attorney-General to institute prosecutions for crimes which have a tendency to disturb the peace of the state or to endanger Government. Therefore the prosecution is really instituted in England by the Attorney-General and not by any private or irresponsible person. Therefore I earnestly draw the attention of the Government to this point, Sir, that when you are undertaking a prosecution, of an offence which is directed against the State or the Government, it must have the previous sanction of a responsible body before such a case can be launched against any citizen; and in my opinion either it must be done with the previous sanction of the Advocate-General or with the previous sanction of the Local Government or the Government of India, and not otherwise.

Therefore, I say that this safeguard is absolutely necessary. The main object of this statute as I said before is to deal with offences against the state. When you are dealing with a Bill of this character, I submit, Sir, that two or more persons is much too small a number. It cannot be a conspiracy of any importance in which there are only two persons connected. You will generally find in conspiracies that are of any really serious character there are more than two persons, and therefore I say the number two is much too small and is likely to cause mischief in practice; you have got the definition of an unlawful assembly; and there you find mention of five or more persons. Therefore I say that you should increase the number to five or more persons. I think you will find that in the case of certain serious offences in England, a conspiracy of three or more persons is referred to. Here it ought to be at least five or more persons and not only two. These are the suggestions I would make, namely section 10 of the Evidence Act to be considered, then you have the explanation to clause 120-A, then you have the manner of prosecution. It would not be allowed unless it has the previous sanction of the Governor-General in Council or the Local Government, or the Advocate-General. Then I say that the number should be five or more persons and not as it stands now as two.

With these remarks, Sir, I will again say that this is a very serious moment—a moment at which I do not think it would be right for us in any way to embarass the Government, but there is one thing which I wish to say that just as there are in India certain people who are responsible for a great deal of mischief so you have certain people who claim to be supporters of or belong to the rank and file of Government who are also responsible for a great deal of mischief, I wish to draw attention to what I read in a newspaper the other day, and that is an extract from the *London Times*—a paper that calls itself the leading paper in Europe. The heading is "Congress party and sedition" "Drastic proposals offered." I will read an extract and the Council will allow me to ask how a paper of this standing, a paper of this character should allow an article so ill-considered or so ill-advised and calculated to hurt the feelings of many of us in India, who, I assure you, Sir, are as anxious to maintain the authority of the Government of India and are as anxious to maintain the law and order as any member of the Government present here.

The article is levelled against those stalwart men, those patriots who head the Congress and have been serving their country. I say, Sir that I am proud that I belong to the Congress Party. That such an article should be written with those insinuations and these aspersions is likely to cause as much mischief as anything that I can think of. The article runs as follows :—

CONGRESS PARTY AND SEDITION.

Drastic Proposals Offered.

Strong Comments in "Times".

A London cablegram says :—" An article in the March number of the *Round Table* on the Delhi outrage, argues that "as the Nationalist leaders' opposition to the Government influences the extremists in the direction of political crimes, the leaders themselves must seek out the sources of conspiracy and prevent their further activity, otherwise the Government may be compelled to say that if political murders recur all representative institutions must be suspended".

The Times says :—The threat of suspension is obviously impossible. It would not be fair to ask the constitutional politicians of India to join in a hunt for the criminals, but it is reasonable to tell them that they cannot for ever evade responsibility, if by opposition they even unconsciously foment disorder, which finds expression in crime. They must either modify their attitude or do something more than express pious horror when outrages occur. By precept and active influence they must set themselves to create a strong feeling of antagonism to conspiracy and must inculcate the duty of helping the Government to detect the offenders. Should they continue to fail in these responsibilities, the verdict must go against them, and anyhow it may be safely said that there can be no further extension of political reform in India while anarchism remains unextirpated'. The *Times* adds: 'We are not satisfied that the duty of repressing crime in India is at present efficiently performed though whether the fault lies chiefly with India or England is open to question. The fact that India is only now bringing its law of Political conspiracy into line with Briton shows that the element of precaution has been lacking. Much more might have been done if the police had been better supported and shielded from undeserved attack, if criminals have been caught red-handed and received swift and sharp punishment if the scandals of interminable political trials had been summarily rectified, and if foolish and mistaken clemency had been less frequent'.

'Now, Sir, the threat is held out to us that we must find out the culprit. If we do not find out the culprit our political institutions must be suspended.'

The President: I am very loath to interrupt the Hon'ble member but he has quoted a document which is not a Government document and one which is in no way pledges the Government or the policy of the Government.

The Hon'ble Mr. Jinnah :—Yes Sir, I know that but I only wish to point out that there is this kind of mischief going on. My appeal to Government is this—I want the Government to take and give expression to the views, that just as you wish us to co-operate with you just as you expect us to stand by you, in the same way you must stand by us and condemn those who are creating this mischief—Just as you condemn those among us who are guilty of misdeeds just as you expect us to join and co-operate with you in condemning our own men who are guilty of misdeeds so you must condemn your men who are also guilty of misdeeds. That is a point which I wish to make clear and that is the reason why I am drawing the attention of the Council to the writings of what is known as the Leading journal in England. With these remarks I have no alternative but to support the principle of the Bill and I trust it will emerge from the Select Committee in a manner that will not go beyond the English law and that the safeguard I have indicated will be provided for.

INDIAN DEFENCE FORCE BILL

The following is the text of the speech of the Hon'ble Mr. Jinnah in the Imperial Legislative Council (February 1917) on the Indian Defence Force.

"My Lord, I welcome this Bill, and I do so for two or three principal reasons. The first reason, My Lord, that strikes me is this, that after the Mutiny the policy of the Government, as has been pointed out over and over again, was regulated (I am not going into the reasons for it) to a certain extent on grounds of distrust of the people, and this Bill is an indication that that policy, rightly or wrongly pursued, has from this day disappeared, from this country. The second ground is, that it opens a door to a service, which was closed to the people of this country except sepoys for all these years under British rule. My Lord, this Bill, I understand that the object of this Bill, is to give an opportunity to the educated people of this country for the defence of their own country. I can assure you, My Lord, knowing as I do know, and I can say that I am in touch with the opinion of Young India particularly, that this measureis welcome. But although as a first step this measure is welcome just as Your Lordship said and you were good enough to take us into your confidence, I think, I ought to tell the Council also in straight language and without mincing matters, that if you want young Indians, if you want educated young Indians to come forward and enlist themselves in the defence of their country, one fact must not be forgotten, and that is the status and privileges which should be given to them. It might be said, 'How is it possible just now for us to give you the commissioned ranks?' I grant it is not possible to do so at once. But there must be a clear indication; that in course of time, it will be granted, I see that is a war measure, which is going to be a war measure, will not be done away with after the war, but it will grow, it will develop, and it will develop into what we have been asking for, namely a national army.

My Lord, it has been said that the people of India have not felt the realities of the war.

Why have they not felt the realities of the war? I grant the people of India have not suffered. The blood of the people of India has not been moved, although there is no doubt that India has done a great deal—a fact which has been very kindly recognised by Your Excellency, by His Excellency the Commander-in-Chief and the Great Ministers in England. But why has not India felt it or not felt it as England feels it? My Lord, the reason is very obvious, and that reason is this, that to-day in England there is not a family that has not lost a son, or a brother or a husband. We, the educated classes in India, have not had the opportunity given to us of losing a son or a husband or a brother. It is for that reason that India has not felt, has not suffered as England has suffered. Who is responsible for this?

My Lord, speaking to Your Excellency and to the Government of India in this Council, I venture to say that it has been now fully realised that India is loyal to the core to the Empire. If India had those opportunities given to it, India would have been a source of great strength to the Empire at this moment; but, unfortunately, we have not had those opportunities.

My Lord, this war has shown clearly that the time has come for a policy of trust in the people of India, and this Bill is a precursor of this policy. I assure you, My Lord, that whatever dissatisfaction, whatever discontent you may observe, that dissatisfaction and that discontent is not due to disloyalty, but it is due to grievances which ought to be attended to and removed. My Lord, with these few remarks, I welcome this Bill, and I sincerely trust, in framing these rules and regulations, some indication will be given to the people of this country that the character, the tone and the organisation, the status and privileges, will be secured to the people of this country which are now secured to European British subjects.

There is one more thing, My Lord, that I should like to impress upon His Excellency the Commander-in-Chief—and I entirely endorse the remarks of the Hon. Mr. Shafi—and that is, that it is absolutely necessary that similar opportunities to those given to European British youths should be given to Indian boys between the ages of 16 and 18 for local service. My reasons are that service, rendered during the period of the war, will prepare these young men for the future army. There is not the slightest doubt that our frontiers have to be guarded; conditions are changing; events are moving rapidly. I do not wish to enter into details at this juncture; but suffice it to say that if anything untoward happens, it would be impossible in the present condition of our army to make an adequate defence of this country. What I call a national army, I venture to say, must come, and the sooner it comes the better—a national army not in the sense that it will be entirely a paid army; there must be a reserve and militia behind it.

My Lord, we know from the experience of this war, how essential it is to have an adequate number of officers. It is a well known fact that, in the Indian army, we have got just enough officers, and if any calamity comes there will be such a paucity of officers that it will be very difficult to manage our affairs.

Therefore, I strongly urge that Indian boys between the ages of 16 and 18 should be given an opportunity of local military service during the period of the war, and, when the bigger question comes to be considered, this will be the material ready to a certain extent having undergone a certain amount of training already, and therefore fit for the future formation of a national army.

IMPERIAL BUDGET 1917—1918.

The following is the text of the Hon. Mr. Jinnah's speech at the Imperial Legislative Council (23rd March 1917) on the Imperial Budget.

"My Lord, it has been said that some of the Members instead of discussing the Budget strictly have diverted from it and discussed all sorts of other matters of public interest. But, My Lord, I have tried to understand the position of a non-official member in this Council. Under our procedure, the Financial Statement is presented, in the first instance, by the Hon. the Finance Member, which was done on this occasion on the 1st of March. After that Financial Statement is presented, no discussion is allowed with regard to the general financial policy of the Government. But those Members who have followed the rules, and I have no doubt that most of the Hon. Members have followed them do find that you can bring in Resolutions with regard to certain matters only, but you cannot possibly discuss in this Council the general financial policy of the Government of India, but that occasion arises after the event, so to say. Therefore, to discuss the Budget at this juncture, it seems to me, will be really flogging the dead horse because not a single item, not a rupee or pie, as far as I understand, can be changed now so far as the Budget is concerned. It does not matter what arguments, what reasons or grounds you advance. Therefore, My Lord, it seems to me that not much good will result by one taking up the Budget at this juncture and discussing it. But I would like to say this for this reason, that when this Financial Statement was introduced by the Hon. the Finance Member, I paid as much attention to it as I could, and personally I came to the conclusion that it was a well-balanced Budget. I think the Hon. the Finance Member has received so many congratulations and so many expressions of gratitude that he might well dispense with any such expression from me. But I do say this, that it was a scientific Budget and what I feel, My Lord, is this, that, as we go on, the Budget will have to be prepared more and more on scientific principles and not in the orthodox way, as one of the Members was pleased to describe it.

Now, with regard to the hundred millions which India has agreed to contribute, I take this view, My Lord, that, if I, as a component of the British Empire, as a citizen of the British Empire, if I can stand here and urge upon the Government that the rights and privileges of a British citizen should be given to me I think I ought to be equally ready to bear the burden of the Empire. There may be differences of opinion on certain matters; and therefore, My Lord, I can tell you this, that on behalf of the people of Bombay, heavy as this burden is, it has been equitably distributed. Of course my friend Mr. Wacha has said that we must not talk about sacrifices; but, My Lord, we are not talking about the sacrifices and the heavy burden in any grudging spirit but in this spirit that the sacrifice is a heavy thing, that is to say, a person who can afford to pay four thousand million can pay four thousand million and suffer less than another person who cannot afford to pay a hundred million. Therefore, when we talk of India's burden and sacrifice, it is only really in that spirit that we speak and in no other spirit, and I am sure that the Government realise it, and I am quite sure that the people in England realise it.

Then, My Lord, with regard to the sources of taxation that have been tapped as I said, we were not in a position to suggest any improvements in the Budget; we were not consulted really on the Budget, and it requires really very, very careful consideration before one can say that you can improve upon this Budget. I dare say it can be improved. But what I would suggest, My Lord, is this, that if there was some such system—a small committee may be formed—we have for instance in Bombay a Finance Committee with a view to discuss the policy of the Budget before the Financial Statement is prepared, I have no doubt that the Government will receive a certain amount of help and that the Hon. the Finance Member will benefit by it.

Well then, My Lord, that is so far as the Budget itself is concerned, but I must say that on this occasion it will be impossible really, as I said, to discuss the Budget only, and the reason, My Lord, that I want to address the Council at this late stage is this. I am fully aware that most of the Members must be thoroughly tired and so is Your Lordship, but there are, My Lord, one or two points which I want to bring to the notice of this Council. The first point, My Lord, is this in regard to the Indian Defence Force Act. The Indian Defence Force Act has become law; it is now more than three weeks, nearly a month, and when it was introduced and when it went through various stages and eventually it was passed, it has raised, as your Lordship must have observed, very great hopes in the minds of the people all over the country and it seems to me, My Lord, that the question is being neglected. First of all, all that we may now know is that anyone who wants to enlist himself can fill up the form, send it to the District Magistrate and it will be sent up in due course to the military authorities and they will do what is required. Now, My Lord, if we are really in earnest, if this door is going to be thrown open to the people of India, and if really the Government of India desires recruits, then I say, My Lord, we shall have to resort to more businesslike methods than I can see up to the present moment. I would, therefore, suggest that the Commander-in-Chief, or whoever is responsible for this, should lose no time, because if you raise the hopes very high and then this measure is misunderstood and it is found that your attention was different from what we understood, there will be bitter disappointment which will be undesirable. Therefore, My Lord, if you are really in earnest, if you really want recruits, and I venture to say you can get recruits by the thousand, thousands provided two or three matters are made clear. It might be said that I am speaking in a spirit of bargaining as it was said the other day. My Lord, any member or anybody who uses that word bargaining, I must say with due respect to him, that he does not realise the true meaning of the word bargaining. All that we urge upon the Government of India is this, there is at the present moment a bar to the people of India so far as the commissioned ranks are concerned. Is it bargaining, consistently with my self-respect as King's equal subject in my own country, to tell my Government face to face that this bar must be removed? Is it bargaining, My Lord, to say that in my own country, I should be put on the same footing as the European British subjects? Is that bargaining? And I say, My Lord, that the sooner this question is taken up the better. There is a very, very strong feeling on this point and if this is put right, I can assure you, My Lord, that you will get thousands of young educated men who will be willing to come forward in the service of their country and the Empire. As I say, My Lord, if that is made clear and if we are in earnest, bureaus must be established in various centres in each Presidency, and we must be told authoritatively how many thousand men we want, and I assure you, My Lord, you shall have them. And when you have these various bureaus established in various centres, appoint some responsible men as the committees, because you will have applicants coming in. I do not wish, My Lord, to strike a note of an offensive character against that service which, in its own way, is doing useful work, namely, the Police and the Criminal Intelligence Department, but, My Lord, as far as possible, that agency should be avoided, and the Police and the Criminal Intelligence Department should have nothing to do with the question of who should be accepted and who should not be accepted.

Then, My Lord, there is one other matter that I wish to refer to and that is this. I was really grieved to hear my Hon. friend, Mr. Shafi, say that if we discuss or ask for any constitutional reforms, that will be embarrassing the Government. What surprises me, My Lord, is this, that my own countrymen should feel more as to what would embarrass the Government than the Government themselves. Why does Mr. Shafi say that respectfully pointing out in this Council that such and such things should be done is going to embarrass the Government? My Lord, Your Lordship was good enough to refer to that memorandum which I venture to say, as I was one of the signatories, was a well-considered and well-thought-out memorandum, and Your Lordship was pleased to say that it would receive sympathetic consideration. My Lord, to that extent I personally say that at the present moment we cannot expect anything more. But, My Lord, that is the fear we have and I want to bring it to the notice of the Government and of Your Lordship. The fear we have is this. The Despatch from the Government of India has gone to the Secretary of State. We do not know what that Despatch contains; we have not the faintest idea. Is the occasion going to be arrived at *ex parte*, give us the opportunity of discussing the matter, and I would suggest (it is only a suggestion just as the Hon. Pandit Madan Mohan Malaviya suggested) I would suggest, My Lord, that, whatever reply may be given to that Despatch before you finally decide on this most vital question, give sufficient opportunity to at least allow the representatives of the people to confer with you a round table before you finally come to any decision, and also give the public an opportunity to criticise it. Is that, My Lord, asking too much, that we should have our representatives consulted with regard to what reforms are going to be introduced? Is that asking for too much? Is it fair that the Government of India in their secret Chambers at Simla or Delhi should form their own opinions and submit a Despatch to the Secretary of State for India, and that the whole question of the post-war reforms should be decided *ex parte* without any body on the part of the people of India being represented or being heard by them? If, My Lord, those reforms are going to be real reforms, I take it that it is a very ordinary proposition that any statesman who wants to introduce any reforms will at least provide for a quarter of a century or half a century, because you cannot go on tinkering with your constitution every five or every ten years. Therefore, My Lord, it is a matter of the most vital importance to India that these questions ought to be considered most seriously and most carefully.

Then, My Lord, there is only one more point while I am talking about reforms, of which your Lordship must be aware, because, it has been repeatedly expressed in the papers, and that is, that if there is going to be an Imperial Council or an Imperial Parliament must be adequately represented. You will ask me perhaps what I mean "adequately represented." My Lord, that is a question which requires detailed consideration, but I can say this at least at once that India's representation in this Imperial Parliament or Imperial Council should certainly be no less than any of the Dominions.

Then, My Lord, there is only one more thing that I want to point out, and that is this. You have been thanked, My Lord, and I entirely join in these thanks to your excellency, for taking the steps that you have under the Defence of India Act for stopping indentured labour. I do not wish, My Lord, to repeat what the other Members have said. But I can tell Your Lordship this that it has given the utmost satisfaction throughout the country; and the people of India do not feel more with regard to any other question than this question of indentured labour for the simple reason that it was degrading, that it was a system not only in itself saturated with evils, but it helped to dishonour a civilised country like India that we should have such a system as the indentured labour system. That, My Lord, was the feeling which really was at the bottom of this strong agitation which Your Excellency must have observed.

In conclusion, My Lord, I will say this, that the standard made by the Secretary of State for India with regard to the cotton duties has created one impression on my mind, and I believe that is the impression created on the minds of a very large section of the thoughtful educated people of this country, namely, that our battle was fought by the Secretary of State for India, who although he had no knowledge or experience of this country, although an Englishman by birth, in spirit fought for us as our Government. And this is what is wanted. The personnel of the Government of this country, as Mr. Gokhale said very often, is foreign. It does not require any argument to establish that. But, My Lord, if you want India to care for your Government, to stand by you, to co-operate with you, what you want is that the spirit of the Government should be Indian, and that on occasions when the interests of India are likely to suffer any injustice is going to be done our Government and those who are at the head of the Government should stand up for us and speak for us as any Indian would do. And, My Lord, Mr. Chamberlain did that, and, therefore, we find this feeling of profound satisfaction. This, My Lord, is all that I have to say and I would urge again upon Your Excellency most earnestly and most sincerely that, with regard to the Indian Defence Force Act, Your Excellency will bear it in mind. I say that, if the Government are in earnest, we are in earnest. We are ready, My Lord, but treat us as the King's equal subjects.

PRIMARY EDUCATION.

The following is the text of the speech of the Hon Mr. Jinnah in the Imperial Legislative Council held on 28th February, 1917, on Primary Education.

The question before the Council, Sir, is put in a particular form as it is embodied in the Resolution, and, although there are some difficulties in agreeing with the actual form in which this Resolution is before the Council I may tell the Council that I am in entire agreement with the spirit of this Resolution, and, I think, there is nobody in this Council among the non-official members who can be of any other opinion. We whole-heartedly sympathise with the spirit of this Resolution.

But there are one or two difficulties which I personally could have appreciated, so far as the Government is concerned, if that attitude had been taken up by the Government at present in not accepting it. But the attitude tàken up by the Hon. Sir Verney Levett, as I understood it from his speech, I hope is not really the attitude of the Government of India, and I also hope that it is not the attitude of even the Government of the United Provinces. Now what does the Hon. Mr. Levett state? He has brought forward an argument, an argument which is as old as the hills. He says there are two difficulties, so far as I could understand him, which he calls administrative difficulties. And what are those two difficulties? The one is that, first of all, you might have to persuade the masses and convince these people, and if you did not do so, there might be riot or 'tumult'—I think that is the word he used. The second was that you would have to employ subordinate officials who will have to enforce compulsion upon the people of those classes, namely, the labourers and the agriculturists and thus may oppress them.

(Here the Hon. Sir Verney Levett rose to a point of order and explained what he exactly meant).

I am much obliged to the Hon. Member for restating what he said. I understood him in the same way, and if he would have had a little patience I think he would have heard my answer to it. The argument is that it does not matter what you do, if you introduce the compulsory system there will be a certain amount of oppression. Will the Hon. Member explain to me when the time will come when you will be in the position to adopt a system without oppression? Is it possible for any Government, if compulsion is going to be introduced, to carry it out except through the subordinate officers? Is it possible to do in any other way? Has it ever been done in any other country in any other way? Is that an argument to advance here in this Council to-day, and, say that our demand for compulsion cannot therefore be responded to? I think it is entirely wrong. That argument is as old as the hills, and I think it is out of place in the twentieth century to advance an argument of this character—that you will have to employ subordinate officials who will oppress the people.

Then the second argument is, I say, equally fallacious, and equally an argument which tends to show that you want to evade the question, *i.e.*, that argument that you must persuade and convince these ignorant people, namely, the labourers and the agriculturists. How many centuries, Sir, shall we be kept waiting for these ignorant illiterate people to be convinced that compulsory education is really for their benefit? I submit, Sir, that both these arguments are fallacious and have no place in the twentieth century when we are discussing a system of compulsory education; and I sincerely hope that that is not the view either of the Government of the United Provinces or the Government of India.

Then the only other expression of opinion that we have got to-day from the other side is that of Sir Sankaran Nair, who represents the Government of India. Now, Sir Sankaran Nair's answer throws the burden on us. He says :—A particular measure was brought before this Council in 1912 by the Hon. Mr. Gokhale; the conditions have not changed since then; we did not accept that measure at the time, how is it possible for us to accept this Resolution now? So far as that argument is concerned, Sir, I admit that there is some apparent force in it; but may I point out to the Hon. Member in charge of the Education Department that the grounds that we urged at that time still hold good, and although Mr. Gokhale's Bill was rejected as the Council is perhaps aware—at least most of the Members are aware—that Sir Harcourt Butler, who was then in charge of the Education Department, gave a reply which was most sympathetic and encouraging. I propose to read the last few sentences of his speech presently. The principal grounds upon which Sir Harcourt Butler then thought that the Government were not in a position to accept that Bill, were, first of all, the financial question; secondly, want of teachers; and thirdly, school buildings. May I, therefore, ask the Hon. Member is it fair to ask us whether those conditions have changed or whether they have not changed? Or is it not more fair that we should ask the Hon. Member, with reference to those difficulties which you pointed out to us five years ago, what you have done during these five years to alter those conditions? And, therefore, personally, Sir, I expected the Hon. Member to tell us how far these three main difficulties that existed five years ago have been removed. We expect the Government to say that they have, in accordance with the promise given by Sir Harcourt Butler, made progress and are in entire sympathy with us, and having made this progress the time has come when they may be able to introduce compulsion. Instead of that, the Hon. Member asks us bluntly to show him what changes have occurred. Well he has got the second right of speech, and I, hope that he will tell me what the Government of India, whose duty it is, have done within the last five years to remove the difficulties that existed five years ago. Sir Harcourt Butler on that occasion said :—

"In time it can create greater adaptability to agricultural and industrial advancement. It can enlarge the minds and brighten the outlook of the people and foster progressive desire which is the root of economic wealth of the community. These are many difficulties ahead, but we shall not flinch. We shall not falter on the way. Though our views may differ as to means, we are all united as to the end. The Government of India, Local Governments, the Departments of Public Instruction and enlightened public opinion are single-eyed as to the end in view. We are determined, resolutely determined, to combat ignorance through the length and breadth of this ancient land, up and down, to and fro; and though the struggle may be long and arduous, I do believe with all my heart, I do believe, we shall prevail.'

Now, Sir, I should like to know from the Hon. the Education Member what he has done in pursuance of this solemn announcement which was made five years ago by the Government. I sincerely hope that at least some progress is made towards reaching that end which we have so dearly at our heart, namely, to combat ignorance through the length and breadth of this ancient land.

SIMULTANEOUS EXAMINATIONS.

The following is the full text of the Hon'ble Mr. Jinnah's speech at the Imperial Legislative Council (21st September, 1917,) on the resolution re-Simultaneous Examinations for the Indian Civil Service in India and England.

Sir, the position that has been taken up by the Hon. the Home Member is one, which, I must say, has not satisfied me. The Hon. the Home Member has pointed out every possible argument that he could lay hold of against simultaneous examinations. Having done that he wound up by saying, very ingeniously, very cleverly, that the Government do not commit themselves in any way at all. Well, if the Hon. the Home Member has taken the trouble to solve all these difficulties,—I have no doubt that he as one of the Members of the Executive Council will put all those difficulties before the Executive Council,—I have no doubt that to a certain extent he has given an indication of his own opinion. I would never have taken part in this debate, but since the Hon. the

Home Member has invited the opinions of non-official members I would like to meet those difficulties. First of all, the Hon. Mr. Atkins said that we never put forward reasons for simultaneous examinations, but he never put forward any against it except one which my Hon. friend Mr. Sastri has dealt with. Now, Sir, I do not wish in any way to convey any idea of criticising the Civil Service unnecessarily. The position is this. The people of India say 'you lay down any test you like, but give us equal opportunities.' Why should the people of India not have equal opportunities? Now, it has been said that the competitive test is the best possible test that we can think of, and I propose, with the permission of the Council, to quote the words of Mr. Balfour which I had the honour of putting forward before the Public Services Commission. This is what Mr. Balfour says:—

'There can be no doubt for example that a man who can succeed in a severe competition must have great powers of work, great powers of concentration, great powers of maturing a subject and great powers of reproducing his knowledge. The existence of these mental powers is shown to demonstration by success and they are all of them of the utmost use in every walk of life and not the least perhaps in that of the Indian Civilian.'

"Now the first difficulty which the Hon. Member puts forward is that it would certainly not maintain the preponderance of the British element. Now, Sir, may I know why is it necessary to have a preponderance of the British element? Why? If, as we are contemplating, we are not going to have, I hope, for a very long time a bureaucracy that will be the servants of the people, and that is what we are aiming at, and if our hopes are realised in the reconstruction of the Government, we hope that the bureaurācy which under the present constitution are the masters and the rulers, will be the servants responsible to the people and under the control of the people. If that is to be realised, may I, Sir, know why there should be a substantial element of the British? We want a service, we want men who will serve us, who will discharge their duties efficiently and faithfully to the Government. I have always failed to understand this argument.

The Hon. Member said well, now, supposing you have to send men to the North-Western Frontier, what will be the position? If you have a Brahmin he may be very efficient as a literary man, full of knowledge. In other words, he conveyed that a Brahmin, if he got into the Civil Service, would be nothing but a bookworm and would not be a man possessing manly qualifications.

(The Hon. Sir William Vincent: 'Indeed, I said nothing of the kind.')

May I know what the Hon. Member meant. Why should not a Brahmin who has passed the test laid down, any test you like educational, physical or otherwise, — why, should not a Brahmin who has passed that test be put in charge of any Province or any district; will the Hon. Member explain that? What will happen to the North-Western Frontier if he goes there? The Hon. Member says, 'Oh! the man with any property if he was living there would at once convert his property into a portable state.' If the Hon. Member is so much afraid of a Brahmin he may be sure the residents of North-Western Frontier will also obey his orders. But, Sir, I go further, how are these provinces now managed by the Civil Servants? We know perfectly well, Sir, that in these Provinces the people are more or less not civilised, people who do not obey the law in the same way as the civilised parts do. We know, Sir, military officers have been sent, military officers have been governing those Provinces, even the Punjab was a non-regulated Province for a very long time and surely such Provinces as are of that character can always be managed by other officers who would be able to prevent the residents of those Provinces from turning their property into a portable state.

I have mentioned the two arguments, namely, preponderance and the question of Provinces such as Burma and the North-West Provinces. The other argument was that we have got in this country different classes of people such as the Muhammadans, Hindus, Parsis, Sikhs and so on, and the Hon. Member quoted certain figures with regard to examinations in the Finance Department as I understood and with regard to the Civil Service Examinations that have been held in London. Well, now, Sir, on this point my answer is this. A man like the late Mr. Dadabhai Naoroji who represents the Parsi community, a man like the late Mr. Gokhale who represents Indians, men like Sir Pherozeshah Mehta who represents the Parsis and men like His Highness the Aga Khan who, as we all know, carried enormous weight with Muhammadans, they all gave their evidence before this very Commission, urging upon the Commission that they wanted simultaneous examinations. Now, Sir, are the opinions of such men not to be taken into consideration. Did they not know the interests of their own communities? The Hon. Member has given figures; he says the result would be that probably the Muhammadans would not get their proper share. Well, Sir, I can tell you this that the Muhammadans are to-day in a much better position than perhaps the Hon. Member knows and are quite prepared to compete with their Hindu brethren, and therefore there need be no anxiety of any kind whatsoever on the part of Government for the Muhammadans. I grant that we are backward to a certain extent, I grant that there is a large number of Hindus in this country than Muhammadans, but assuming a larger number of Hindus do get into the Civil Service will that be more objectionable to the Muhammadans than that a larger element of the Europeans should get in? I want to be frank. I do not want to give any offence, but why should it be any more objectionable to the Muhammadans if the Hindus are more than if the Europeans are more? There I say that is an argument which I submit has no place here. What we want, Sir, is this, we want an efficient service. Let it be open to competition to any one, to Europeans, Hindus and Muhammadans, Parsis, etc. and the fittest get in, the survival of the fittest should be the rule for recruiting the highest service.

Then I give you what my objections are at the present moment to the Civil Service examination being held in London only. Sir, we know perfectly well, and let me tell you this that the Indian element which you now get by this door, which is a door which really more obstructs the Indians from getting in because you put so many difficulties in the way, a man has got to go to London, a man who has to get money, a man who has to take the chance and the risk of working for years and at the end of 5 or 6 years, if he fails in the Civil Service, he is good for nothing.

(The Hon. Sir William Vincent. "I always understood he went to the Bar.")

No, the Hon. Member is very much mistaken. If he cannot get into the Civil Service he will be much less able to get on at the Bar. However that is beside the point. Therefore you expect people to go to London all the way taking all these risks and then at the end find themselves, if failures, with nothing to do. On the other hand if you had simultaneous examinations in this country you would find better men, better talents will have an opportunity of competing and you will get better men, I venture to say better men will get in, if you had examinations here in India as well as in London. Therefore, Sir, I strongly object to the present system of recruiting for the Civil Service, and I say that it is obvious to any thinking man that, while theoretically the Civil Service examination is open to the sons of India, practically every possible difficulty is put in their way and the result of that is that you find (I believe that I am right) that out of 1,300 Civilians holding various posts in this country to-day there are no more than 60 or 70 Indians. Well, that is the state of things, that although in theory it is open to His Majesty's subjects in India to compete for the Civil Service, to all practical purposes, the door is really closed.

Now we say open that door properly and let there be honest equal competition. Let the best talent of India compete for it. Put any test you like, and then whoever is the fittest should get into that service. I do not see any reason against it or any objection to or any answer to that proposal. Therefore, I would ask the Hon. Mover to divide the Council on this Resolution and let us record our most emphatic opinion on this Resolution by our vote.

INDIAN CIVIL SERVICE.

The following is the text of the speech of the Hon. Mr. Jinnah in the Imperial Legislative Council (24th September, 1917) on the Resolution re. Proportion of Indian Recruits in the Indian Civil Service.

It is but right that this Council should consider the alternative and express its opinion whether the alternative should be accepted or not. Well, the only objections that have been raised against this alternative are the same objections, *viz*, that if 50 per cent. of Indians get into the Indian Civil Service it would imperil the British character of the administration. Well, Sir, I want to know what is meant by the "British character of the administration." Is the meaning of this phrase, European element? Is the meaning of this phrase, colour? Or is the meaning of this phrase those great qualities which have distinguished the European administrators of this country? Is the phrase 'British character of the administration' means those great qualities, *viz.*, uprighteousness, honesty, integrity, high sense of duty,—and I have no hesitation in acknowledging that many members of the Civil Service have displayed them in this country—I can understand it. If an Indian also has those qualities and if such Indians are the preponderating element in the Civil Service, does that mean British character of administration or not? Or must it mean that we must have so many of a particular race or colour? If latter is the meaning, Sir, I strongly object to such a rule or standard. No race, no question of religion or creed has to be considered in recruiting our highest service. Efficiency is the only test and those qualities which I have mentioned above.

I come next to the argument of the commercial classes which my Hon. friend Mr. Hogg represents. I have got very great respect for Mr. Hogg, Sir, and I know that he holds very liberal views. But I was really surprised that he should have brought in the question of passive resistance as an instance of how the commercial community might suffer. With very great respect for him, I submit that it is not only irrelevant, but if it had any relevancy of talk at all, one might retort and say that some of the Anglo-Indians at the present moment notably '*Madras Mail*' are preaching and are guilty of insubordination. But those questions really must not be mixed up with this question before us to-day. How is the commercial interest going to suffer? If you have men who are competent and properly qualified in the service, how is the commercial interest going to suffer because they happen to be Indians. After all, it is nothing but the service we are recruiting, and why should there be any danger to the commercial community? What is going to happen to the commercial interests, I have not yet heard of. We know perfectly well that British capital is invested and employed in many parts of the world including India. For example, you have a large amount of British capital in South Africa where there is an overwhelming majority of Boers; and as a matter of fact, we know that soon after the war broke out there was a great deal of disturbance there."

Sir, as regards British capital, if this argument is to stand good what is and what will be the result? British capital on the one side but what is it after all as against the enormous interests and stake of the people of this country, and of the sons of this country? What is this British capital that is trotted out over and over again? Are the interests of the people of India not to be considered? If you are going to apply this test of British capital in this country to maintain preponderating element of Europeans in the service, why will doomsday you will never get over it. For when will the British capital disappear from India—God forbid I do not wish it to disappear. I trust that more may come in. But if that argument is to stand good for having preponderating element of Europeans then I say there will never be a change. I ask, Sir, is that logical? I would answer and say that this argument is fallacious. All that we want is that the services may be recruited properly and efficiently. It is for this reason that Europeans are employed as foreign skill: but once you get the sons of the country who are capable and competent there is no justification for maintaining that there should be a certain number of Europeans. Therefore, Sir, I have no alternative but to support this resolution. I must say that I am opposed to any proportion being fixed in favour of Indians or Europeans, Sir, we must have justice. I do not fully agree with any system where a proportion is laid down of any class, but if there is no other way, if there is no other course open, then I would vote for and support this Resolution as an alternative Resolution.

THE INDIAN TRANSFER OF SHIPS RESTRICTIONS BILL.

The following is the text of the Speech of Mr. Jinnah in the Imperial Legislative Council (20th September, 1917) on the Indian Transfer of Ships Restrictions Bill.

"My Lord, it is with some hesitation that I ventured to give notice of the amendment that it stands in my name that in clause 2 (1) (i) after the words and figures 'Aliens Act 1914' the following be inserted: 'and will include Indian subjects of His Majesty,' because I am fully aware that the Legislative Department is very ably represented. However the question is one which I thought, when I received the Agenda, showing that the Hon. Member in charge of the Bill was going to move that it be taken into consideration and passed, should be placed before the Council. The Agenda was received by me only on Monday night, since then I have tried to devote some attention to this question. The matter stands in this way; the definition in the Bill is this, section 2 says :—

'British subject means a person who is a natural-born British subject within the meaning of the British Nationality and Status of Aliens Act of 1914.'

Now, the question is whether that definition will include an Indian subject of His Majesty or not. It seems to me that there is considerable doubt thrown on the point by the Acts of Parliament passed from time to time; for this purpose I will draw the attention of the Council to the observations made by Ilbert in his book. 'The Government of India,' he says on page 379 :—

"It appears to have been held at one time that the expression 'natural-born subjects' is in the statutes affecting India, always taken to mean European British subjects, and although his position can no longer be maintained in its entirety.'

He then refers to some English statutes :—

"There is ground for argument that it may be construed subject to restrictions in its application to descendants of non-European subjects of the Crown."

Then on page 411 this is what he says :—

"Consequently the term 'British subject' has to be construed in a restricted sense in the earlier of the enactments, and it is possible that the restricted meaning which had been attached to it by usage still continued to attach to it when used in some of the enactments dating subsequently to the time when British India had passed under the direct and immediate sovereignty of the Crown. The term as used in Acts of Parliament was never precisely defined and perhaps was treated as including generally white-skinned residents or sojourners in the country by way of contradistinction to the native population"

I am fully aware that the Hon. the Law Member will probably point out to me that if we term to the definition after all this is a definition by reference to the Act of 1914, the words are as follows :—

"The following persons shall be deemed to be natural-born British subjects, namely, any person born within His Majesty's dominions and allegiance."

Now as to the word 'dominions' it may be that the Hon. the Law Member will say that it will include any part of the Empire, and that will include India. The only hesitation which I have in my mind is that we can talk of dominions that generally conveys, that the idea of a self-governing dominion and that does not include India. We have the term in the first place 'British possession' and it is a question whether that term will include India or not. It is for that reason, My Lord, that I want to make it quite clear and so I propose in my amendment the addition of the words and will include Indian subjects of His Majesty'. However I am open to conviction and if the Hon. the Law Member satisfies the Council that the clause does include Indian subjects of His Majesty I am prepared to accept the statement.

My Lord, I want to make one observation that is not quite germane to my amendment ; I do not want to make a second speech. With regard to what fell from the Hon. Member in charge of the Bill I have no doubt that explanation will certainly allay the feelings that were created in Bombay, but I would like to point out that (he referred to apprehensions in the minds of shipowners) the Hon. Member is perhaps aware that when the Act was passed.

THE WORKING OF INDIAN RAILWAYS.

The following is the text of the speech of Mr. Jinnah in the Imperial Legislative Council (25th September, 1917) re. the appointment of a mixed committee to examine the working of the Indian Railways.

Sir, The Resolution which I beg to move runs as follows :—

> "*This Council recommends to the Governor-General-in-Council that a mixed committee be appointed to examine the working of the Indian Railways Act and to make their recommendations at an early date.*"

Now, the Council is perhaps aware that when the Indian Railways Act of 1890, was passed we had two previous English Acts, one was the Act of 1888 and another of 1873. On examining the Indian Railways Act 1890, I find that instead of following the model of the later English law, namely, the Act of 1888 the earlier Act of 1873 has been followed. That is an anomaly, which I have no doubt will be explained by the Hon. Member in charge. But it is quite possible that the reasons were that some of the guaranteed Railways, the Bombay, Baroda and Central India and the Great Indian Peninsula Railways were in different circumstances when the Government framed the Act of 1890. But, Sir, I submit that the time has come for overhauling that Act and particularly the provisions which will place the administration of Indian Railways on a sounder footing. Personally, I would like to see the provision somewhat on the lines of the English Act regarding a permanent Commissioner to hear complaints embodied in the Act. Perhaps the Council is aware that Mr. Robertson was appointed sometime ago to inquire into Railway administration and that after a very careful enquiry he made an important report in 1903. In that report he pointed out that the Railway Commission which is provided for in the Act of 1890 has never been taken advantage of for obvious reason and that under S. 26 of the Indian Railways Act a Commission can only be appointed when asked for by the Governor-General in Council and what is more, it is so expensive, so costly and probably the party asking for a Commission may have to pay the costs. Section 26 of our present Act reads thus :—

'For the purposes of this chapter, the Governor-General in Council shall, as occasion may, in his opinion, require, appoint a Commission styled a Railway Commission (in this Act referred to as the Commissioners) and consisting of one Law Commissioner and two lay Commissioners.'

Then it provides for the costs.

"The costs of and incidental to proceedings before the Commissioners of the High Court under this Chapter shall be in the discretion of the Commissioners or the High Court as the case may be."

The point that I wish to bring to the notice of the Council—I do not wish to go into the details of the constitution of the Commission as provided for in this Act because it is quite unnecessary to go into those details—is that you here have a commission appointed if anybody asks for it, it is not a permanent commission, under the statute, it is not a commission, as I shall point out to the Council, such as we have under the English Act. And, further, the part relating to the costs, is rather an important matter to consider. Now, Mr. Robertson, who as I told the Council before, had gone into this question at great length and this is what he said in his report:—

> "Under the provisions of the present Indian Railways Act, the calling into existence of the Railway Commission to hear complaints against Railways is considered so costly an undertaking that the commission has never once been created."

In his report he also recommended that to afford the public and the Railways the greatest advantages of which the commission is capable, it should be required to hold its courts not only at a few chief centres but where exceptional circumstances arise at the place nearest and most convenient to the complainant, having regard to the general convenience of all others interested. Now the English Act of 1888 provides quite a different machinery, and that is contained in section 2 of the English Railways Act which constitutes the commission. Section 2 runs as follows:—

> 'On the expiration of the provisions of the regulation of Railways Act, 1873, with respect to the commissioners therein mentioned there shall be established a new commission styled the Railway and Canal Commission in this Act referred to as the Commissioners and consisting of two appointed and three *ex-officio* Commissioners, such Commission shall be a court of record.'

Section 5 empowers the Commission to hold sittings in any part of the United Kingdom, and in such place or places as may be most convenient for the determination of the proceedings before them.

Therefore, Sir, what I urge is this, that instead of having a provision such as is contained in our sub-section 26, we ought to have a permanent Commission which will be available to any complainant, and what is more, they can sit in any part of the country where the complaints can be heard and investigated. Mr. Robertson in his report made his recommendation and urged regarding this matter the following point which I shall give in his own words. Paragraph 61 of his report says:—

'The Commissioners in addition to their duties on the Board should be employed in association with a Law Member when a question of Law arises as Commissioners for the purposes of Chapter V. of the Indian Railways Act (IX of 1890) which regularises Railway Commissioners and Traffic facilities *the present Act being revised on the lines of the English Railway and Canal Traffic Act of 1888*, so as to permit of the Railway Commission always being in session.

Another thing that I wish to bring to the notice of the Council is this. At present the control of the Government of India as I understand is *nil* over the Railways. We know that cases are not unknown where the Railway Board have been able to get round the Secretary of State for India in certain matters over the heads of the Government of India. As far as I understand, Sir, the Railway Board is not constituted or established so as to give any control over it to Government under the statute, and the Agent or Traffic Manager of a Railway Company is not in any way subject to the control of the Government of India. I know that there is a Member in the Secretary of State's Council who is called the Railway Director, and through him, no doubt, the Secretary of State is very often approached and influenced, but I have not been able to find out any statutory powers which vests in the Government of India any authority to interfere with the Railway Board or the Agent or the Traffic Manager of any Railway Company. I submit, Sir, that we ought to take more powers, and the Government of India ought to have more control over the Railways than it has at present.

The next point that I wish to bring to the notice of the Council is this. The complaints which I would divide into various heads might be heard by this Commission which I propose should be created by the statute. The complaints would be first of all from commercial and trading firms with regard to rates and with regard to preference which might be given, and in that the commercial community of this country is very much interested. With regard to this complaint it is not unknown that sometimes preference is given and therefore it would be much more satisfactory if any such complaints were made to the Commission which would be an independent tribunal and it would hear both sides, namely, the Railway Company or those representing the company and the complainant.

Then the next item which might be considered is this: Passengers' complaints. With regard to Passengers' complaints we know that it is a very well known fact in India that there is a great deal of overcrowding, which is visible to any casual traveller at any station when travelling, and that is a matter which requires very careful attention and it ought to be put right. Then there are many other matters such as ventilation,lighting,sanitation, and particularly the refreshment rooms. These are only a few suggestions which I want to put before the Council to show why a Comittee should be appointed, and I do not say that every one of these questions will have to be embodied in the Act. These are some of the suggestions that I put before the Council in order to support my resolution that it is time that a committee should be appointed to consider all these questions and make such recommendations as the Committee may think proper with a view to modify the present Act of·1890. Then also the question of public safety may be considered. We know, Sir, that accidents happen and in the case of an accident at present, as far as I have been able to make out, you have merely the Railway officials and somebody representing the Government or the Police. Those are the two bodies who have any voice in the matter of enquiring into any railway accident. There again it is desirable in the case of any serious accident to have some non-official representative at the inquiry. There might be a *punch*, or there might be one or two citizens who should be associated with the Railway authorities, and they should have a voice in the inquiry in the case of any serious accident. At present, the inquiry is made by the Railway authorities and nobody else practically.

Then the next question that is also of great importance is in regard to the railway employees. Now I am not dealing with the bigger employees, nor am I dealing with the clerks and railway officials, but the largest number employed by the Railways belong to the humbler class, namely, the labourers, and so far as those employees are concerned we know there have been strikes, and particularly a strike in Bombay, *viz.*, the Great Indian Peninsula Railway strike. I am quite sure, Sir, that if there was any machinery such as Conciliatory Boards or a Commission which could have inquired into this matter, the strike would not have lasted as long as it did, and it was certainly a tremendous loss to the Railway which is after all a State Railway, and a loss to those poor strikers. Perhaps the Hon. Member knows that outside or private intervention was objected to but eventually His Excellency the Governor of Bombay had to intervene, and it was really that intervention which put an end to that strike. Therefore I say it is absolutely essential that there should be some machinery by which these strikes can be dealt with, and a body which would hold the scales even between the Railway Company and the labourers should be constituted to deal with the matter. In the past, I believe some such procedure was adopted. I think there were strikes in 1906 and 1907, and particularly I may mention the strike which took place on the Eastern Bengal State Railway Company when the drivers and foreman caused a temporary dislocation, and also on the East Indian Railway when the European and Eurasian drivers of Howrah struck, and that really was a very serious strike, and it was only terminated by the appointment, by the Government, of a special Board which dealt with the question of higher pay, of mileage allowance and extra pay for working overtime and on holidays and so on. That was done in the case of the strike in the Howrah on the East Indian Railway line. But there is no provision in the statute for it in India; that was only done to meet that particular case. We know perfectly well that as we go on, although we do not wish to have these troubles and nobody wants these troubles less than I do, we know that the labour question must grow in importance. In England, where labour is so well organised and so powerful you have, notwithstanding that, provisions for dealing with these labour questions. I would draw the attention of the Council to section 31 of the English Act which lays down the provision with regard to complaints to the Board of Trade about unreasonable charges by Railway Companies. I do not wish to trouble the Council by reading the section which also lays down the machinery to deal with complaints about unreasonable charges by Railway Companies. It says :—

'The Board of Trade, if they think there is reasonable ground of complaint, may call upon the railway company for an explanation and endeavour to settle any differences between the complainant and the railway company.'

You also find that, what is more, the Board of Trade,—

'Shall from time to time submit to Parliament reports of the complaints made to them under the provisions of this section, and the results of the proceedings taken in relation to such complaints, together with such observations thereon as the Board of Trade think fit'

Therefore I would submit that in all these matters, not only these complaints and these grievances, if any, put forward should be investigated by a proper body constituted under the statute, but the reports of the proceedings should be submitted to the Imperial Legislative Council.

Well, Sir, these are some of the points which I submit are such as require very careful consideration and hence I submit, Sir, that our Act needs modification and revision. I would therefore ask the Council to accept this Resolution.

Then, as to the constitution of any Committee that might be appointed, to consider these various points, I submit that it should be a small Committee. After all, on most of these points we have the model and the experience of England, and there would not be much difficulty in following that model and experience, save and except in such matters of detail where the circumstances and the conditions of this country are different. Therefore, I would submit, Sir, that a very small committee should be appointed consisting of one member who should represent the commercial class, one member who should represent the travelling public, while the rest of the members of the committee might consist of representatives of the Government and the Railway Companies. But the committee should be as small as possible. Then that committee, if they wanted any information, would take such evidence as they might require or call for such information as they might require on these various questions. The reason that I advocate a small committee is that it would be able to proceed without delay to inquire into the matter and make recommendations.

LEGISLATION IN THE PUNJAB.

The following is the text of the speech of Mr. Jinnah delivered in the Imperial Legislative Council on 12th September, 1917 re. the resolution of the administration and legislative in the system Punjab :—

Sir, as the Resolution is worded, I am afraid I cannot give my support to it. I thoroughly sympathise with its object, which is the limited ambition that the legislative and administrative system of the Punjab should be assimilated to the one which prevails in Bihar and Orissa. Sir, this reform is overdue, and I am glad my Hon. friend the Mover of this Resolution has at last after such a long time realised that his province was not properly treated. But now that he has aroused himself and brought up this Resolution unfortunately he has brought it up at a moment which seems to me wholly inopportune. We know that the general question of constitutional reform, which affects the Province of the Punjab as well as the Government of India, is going to be taken up very soon. We have all seen the pronouncement made by the Secretary of State for India and we know that he is coming out to India for that very purpose. I personally, Sir, have held this view, that the Punjab should have a Governor in Council and not a Lieutenant-Governor. The Hon. Mr. Shafi, however, is much more modest in his views and he says that he will be quite content to get what Bihar has got. I, for one, do not agree with him. I think the Punjab should have a Governor in Council like any other Province, like Bombay or Bengal; and I also go further than the Hon. Mr. Shafi does in another direction. I think the High Court should be under the control of the Government of India, like the High Court of Calcutta. That is a question of the utmost importance, not only to the Punjab but to every other Province, and the sooner the question is seriously taken up the better. I have no doubt that it will be taken up when the general scheme of reform is being discussed. I am, therefore, unable to support the Resolution in the form in which it has been moved. I may tell you, Sir, I may tell the Council here, that considerable misapprehenison has been aroused in the Punjab in view of the form in which the Resolution has been worded and the time at which it is brought before this Council. Several telegrams have reached us in which people have expressed grave apprehension about it. However, the reply which the Hon. the Home Member has given to this proposal will, I have no doubt, satisfy not only the Punjab but the whole of India, namely, that the Government will give it their sympathetic consideration, and, of course, that was the only reply which the Government could have given at this stage. Therefore, the question resolves itself into this, that this question of the Punjab must be taken up along with the general question of the constitutional reforms which should be introduced in India after the war. In these circumstances, I am unable to support the Resolution much as I sympathise with its object. I cannot support it, because it ought to have been brought long ago and the present moment is an inopportune one. Further, the form in which it has been put is not satisfactory, because in my opinion the Punjab should have Governor in Council and a High Court under the control of the Government of India.

POLICE ADMINISTRATION.

The following is the speech of the Hon'ble Mr. Jinnah on the Police administration, on the resolution of the Hon'ble Babu Bupendranath Basu in the Imperial Legislative Council (March 1912.)

Sir, after the speeches that have been made by the Mover and the other Hon'ble Members, there is very little left to be said on this Resolution. I want to make it quite clear to the Council that I do not wish to enter into controversy of either racial, national or personal a character ; and I think it is not desirable that the questions that come before this Council should be viewed from that point of view by any one of this Council. Each question that comes here, comes here for the consideration of the Council on the merits. It is neither a question of English people or Indian people, but it is a question which affects the administration of this country. And we are all here, whether English or Indians, here with one desire, namely, whether there is a particular evil, whether there is a particular system which ought to be altered or the evil ought to be remedied. And, Sir, I am going to deal with the Resolution entirely on the merits of the question and the arguments. The Hon'ble Mr. Basu has given numerous instances pointing out the evils of the system of the Police Administration To those instances I beg the liberty of adding one more, very recent one. In Bombay we had recently a trial of a great nobleman, the Chief of Hoti; what is known as the Hoti Mardan case in Bombay. This gentleman is highly respected in Northern India and, I believe, one of the wealthiest men in his place. Sir, this gentleman was brought down to Bombay on a charge of abduction along with two others. He was placed before the Presidency Magistrate on that charge, and the Presidency Magistrate refused to release him on bail. After the evidence had been completed before the Presidency Magistrate, he, along with two others, was committed to the Sessions Court in Bombay; and after three days of trial the Advocate-General representing the prosecution had to withdraw the prosecution against this gentleman. It came to this, Sir, that the prosecution broke down completely, and I think that it is well known in Bombay, and I think it is also well known in Calcutta, that the presiding Judge made the severest remarks against the police in Northern India. He was surprised that this case should ever have been launched in any Court at all. Now, there it was I think a European police-officer who was responsible for launching the prosecution. Therefore, Sir, it is clear that along with the numerous instances which the Hon'ble Mover has given, and this recent one which seems to me that it has done the grossest injustice to this nobleman, for which I do not know that he has got any remedy that is worth considering. Great evil does exist. Now the question is—what is the cause of it? There must be something wrong somewhere. Therefore is it too much for the Hon'ble Mover to ask this Council to appoint a Commission to inquire into this case? A Commission consisting of officials and non-official members may be able to make very useful and very practical suggestions, which might, if not eradicate the evil altogether, palliate the evils that exist at the present moment.

Therefore, Sir, on these grounds I support that part of the Resolution.

As to the second part of the Resolution, namely, the amendment of the law of confession I have very few words to say. The Hon'ble Mr. Basu, unless I failed to catch him or understand him, did not make the point clear on what part of the law regulating confessions amendments are necessary, and I for one do not know as to which portion of that law requires amendment. I know, Sir, of two recent instances, one I think in the case decided in the Madras High Court, and one instance in Bombay. Of course it is well known that a confession made in the presence of police-officers is inadmissible in evidence. In Bombay, in a case recently, a confession was made to a non-policeman, but a police-officer happened to be standing above on the verandah. The confession was made to a non-policeman down below, and the police-officer came into the witness-box and wanted to give this evidence. It was said that the statement was not made in his presence, he only happened to be on this verandah and overheard the conversation. That was rejected by the Court. Another case was in Madras where it was attempted to have a confession admitted on the ground of corroboration, namely, that you cannot give it in evidence as a confession, but you can give it by way of corroboration. But, Sir, if there was any need to regulate the law relating to confessions of accused persons, it is open, I think, to the Hon'ble Member or to any other Member to bring in a Bill to that effect in this Council or to amend any part of the existing law. And probably if the attention of the Law Member be drawn to the evil, if any, that exists in this respect, I have not the slightest doubt that the Hon'ble the Law Member will be the first to rectify the Law in that direction. But why usurp this Council of its proper functions and leave a matter of this kind to a Commission when we can do that ourselves here? Therefore, Sir, I do not understand the latter part of the Resolution. I support the first part of the Resolution.

INDIAN EXTRADITION BILL.

The following is the text of the speech of the Hon. Mr. Jinnah in the Imperial Legislative Council (March 1913) on the Indian Extradition Amendment Bill:—

Sir, I have listened to the speech of the Hon'ble Member in charge of this Bill with very great attention. I am sorry to say that I was not present when this Bill was introduced at Simla, and also that I was not present when the Bill was referred to Select Committee; therefore, I do not know the stages through which the Bill has gone, and my position is somewhat difficult. That position is made still more difficult by the remark that fell from the Hon'ble the Home Member that the Government had agreed to certain amendments in Select Committee and that further than that they are not prepared to go, so what little hope I had when I entered this Council-hall this morning, is, if I may say so, almost shattered; but I still venture, Sir, to put my views before this Council, and I particularly appeal to the Government and the Hon'ble Member in charge of this Bill. I still hope that after what I shall presently make clear to the Council, he will please consider those points which I want very earnestly to bring to his attention. No doubt, Sir, this Bill, as it was introduced, was certainly not liked in Bombay and the people of Bombay felt that they proposed a change which certainly revolutionized the position of Presidency-towns.

The Hon'ble Member in charge of the Bill said that when the old Bill was passed into law in 1903, it was intended to apply to the whole of British India, but by some kind of slip which we in Bombay thought to be providential the Presidency-towns did not come under the purview of that Bill. The advantage was this: that if a man happened to be in any Presidency-town and if any Foreign State or Native State wanted to extradite that man from any Presidency-town, then a *prima facie* case had to be made out before the Presidency Magistrate. That was an advantage which I can understand, any man may, well prize before he is taken away under arrest by virtue of the warrant into a Foreign State, and before he is handed over to be tried by the judiciary of a Foreign State. And here I may point out this with very very great respect for the Native States: there are Native States and Native States; there are judiciaries and judiciaries. Therefore, Sir, it was a very great advantage to the Presidency-towns. Now it is said: 'But it applies to the districts, and why should a British subject in a Presidency-town have better advantages than other subjects of the British Empire in districts in British India?' Is that any argument, Sir, that because British subjects in the district labour under certain disadvantages, therefore you must bring those disadvantages into Presidency-towns that are labouring under no such disadvantages? That is an argument that does not appeal to me. But, says the Hon'ble Malik of Tiwana, why should the people in Presidency-towns enjoy better advantages than people not in Presidency-towns? My answer would be that they can put that right in the districts, but that is no reason why you should put people in the Presidency-towns under a similar disadvantage. That is hardly an argument. The question really is this. It may be that owing to certain exigencies, owing to certain reasons, the Government may desire to introduce this measure, but it seems to me that on principle, and on principle alone, the effect of this measure will be, so far as the Presidency-towns are concerned, to withdraw the security that we have had hitherto, namely, that before a man is taken away to be tried by any foreign judiciary a *prima facie* case must be made out before a competent, fully qualified and efficient judiciary in any of the Presidency-towns. That privilege is going to be taken away from us. Therefore I regret to say that I do not feel satisfied with this measure. But as I said before I am somewhat late in entering this protest here to-day. Therefore, not being satisfied with this Bill as it stands, I would appeal to Government and the Member in charge to alter the Bill so as not to take away any possible advantage given to us before this Bill was introduced. As the Hon'ble Member pointed out, under sec. 15 of the Extradition Act, Government—either the Government of India or the Local Government—had the power to stay the proceedings and cancel the warrant. That sec. 15 did not provide the methods or the kind of inquiry which should be made before the Government took that step. Under that sec. 15 it seems to me that the Government had ample power to deal with this case; but as the Hon'ble the Home Member has pointed out, that power could have also been exercised by the Presidency Magistrate in this way; he could have made such inquiry himself as he may have thought proper and sec. 15 being quite silent on the point, he could have drawn the attention of Government to the particular case. Under that state of things, it seems to me, Sir, that the Magistrate had much greater powers than the powers given to the Magistrate to-day; because by this amended section 8-A the only power that you are giving to the Magistrate is to record a statement of the accused, if any is made by him, and nothing more: whereas, if I understand the Hon'ble the Home Member correctly, under sec. 15 there was an implied power an implied authority given to the Magistrate to make such inquiries as to him seemed proper and to report to Government. It seems to me, therefore, Sir, that if that is the correct interpretation of sec. 15—about which I personally am very doubtful—then by this amendment which is apparently made with a view to improve the position you are cutting down the discretion and the power of the Magistrate only, and cutting it down and reducing it so that he cannot do anything more than record the statement of the accused person.

Now, Sir, if you are reducing the functions of the Magistrate only to one point, that is to recording the statement of the accused and doing nothing more, I ask, Sir, how is the Magistrate to be in a position to decide whether these cases are to be reported to Government or not. Will the statement of the accused give sufficient material for the Magistrate to make up his mind? Now, Sir, what would happen is this. First of all the inquiry will be made in a Native State that wishes this accused person extradited. That inquiry will consist of nothing else but depositions taken down, I will say by the Political Agent himself. The depositions will be *ex parte* without having gone through the test of cross examination and will take for example that you have half a dozen men who will go and swear on oath before the Political Agent personally and swear to this effect that A has committed a certain offence, namely, criminal breach of trust. The Political Agent has nothing else before him except the depositions of half a dozen men on oath. The chances are hundred to one, I venture to say, that the Political Agent will be bound to issue a warrant, because you have the sworn testimony of half a dozen men before you, nothing to contradict it nothing to test it. And therefore in ordinary cases the odds are a hundred to one the Political Agent will issue a warrant. That warrant now I take it for the purposes of my example goes to Bombay for execution. The accused person, I am calling him A, is arrested in Bombay and placed before the

Presidency Magistrate, he is arrested under warrant and placed before the Presidency Magistrate, to be dealt with under section 7 of the Act. When he is placed before the Magistrate under section 8 A, namely that section which is before the Council, the Magistrate will then record the statement of the accused person and that statement, Sir, I venture to say in 999 cases out of 1,000 would be that he is not guilty, that the charge is a false one. How is the Magistrate to decide whether these cases ought to be reported to Government or not? Is he to rely on the mere *ipse dixit* of the accused person and take the responsibility upon himself to report the case to the Government for inquiry? Therefore, Sir, it seems to me that you are not only restricting the powers of the Magistrate which are vested in him under the old Act but I say that you are restricting the powers of the Magistrate in such a way that it will be impossible for him to make up his mind whether a particular case should be reported to Government or not. You must give him something more than the mere *ipse dixit* of the accused person, so as to enable him as a reasonable man, as a Judicial Official, to make up his mind whether this is a case that ought to be reported to Government or not. For this reason, I am not at all satisfied. As regards the concession, namely, that the Magistrate shall record the statement of the accused person, I say 'leave it out,' I would rather be without it. If you wish to give a proper concession, if you really wish to have a proper safeguard then I say give the Magistrate further powers to record not only the statement of the accused person but such evidence as he may wish to produce. In that case the Magistrate will not only have the statement of the accused person which, remember, is not on oath which, remember, is always discounted and remember, Sir, that the accused person is so interested that his statement is always discounted. The accused person is not likely to make a statement and say 'I am guilty.' The accused person in each case will say that 'the Political Agent is my enemy, that the Durbar are maliciously proceeding against me, that the charge is a false one.'

Therefore I say give the accused person an opportunity if he likes to call such evidence as he may be advised to corroborate his statement. This will give the Magistrate some materials and also provide an opportunity for the accused to argue before the Magistrate those cases that are to be reported to Government for further enquiry. Therefore I would appeal to the Hon'ble Member and I would suggest this amendment of the clause. It would run as follows :—

'8 A. Notwithstanding anything contained in section 7, sub-section (2) or in section 8, when an accused person arrested in accordance with the provisions of section 7 is produced before the District Magistrate or Chief Presidency Magistrate, as the case may be, after the statement (if any) of such accused person has been recorded, and after taking such evidence as may be tendered on behalf of the accused, such Magistrate may, if he thinks fit, before proceeding further, report the case to the Local Government and, pending the receipt of orders on such report, may detain such accused person in custody or release him on his executing a bond with sufficient sureties for his attendance when required.'

I say that the adoption of that would not do any harm to anybody.

That is my suggestion, Sir, and I hope it will be considered and approved by the Council.

INDEX.